DAYS OUT
UNDER
GROUND

For Nicola, Toby and Willow. Thanks for going underground!

CONWAY
Bloomsbury Publishing Plc
50 Bedford Square, London, WC1B 3DP, UK

BLOOMSBURY, CONWAY and the Conway logo are trademarks
of Bloomsbury Publishing Plc

First published in Great Britain 2019

A catalogue record for this book is available from the British Library

Library of Congress Cataloguing-in-Publication data has been applied for

ISBN: PB: 978-1-8448-6567-3
        ePub: 978-1-8448-6566-6
        ePDF: 978-1-8448-6568-0

2 4 6 8 10 9 7 5 3 1

Typeset in The Serif
Designed by Austin Taylor
Illustration by David Broadbent
Printed and bound in China by C&C Offset Printing Co

To find out more about our authors and books visit
www.bloomsbury.com and sign up for our newsletters.

All prices were correct at the time of going to press. We recommend
readers confirm with the attractions before visiting. Contact details
are provided throughout.

DAYS OUT UNDER GROUND

50 SUBTERRANEAN ADVENTURES
BENEATH BRITAIN

PETER NALDRETT

CONWAY

LONDON · OXFORD · NEW YORK · NEW DELHI · SYDNEY

CONTENTS

INTRODUCTION

THE MYSTERY OF WHAT LIES BENEATH our feet has captured the human imagination for millennia. There has always been a fascination with what we'll find when we dig down into the ground, how the raw materials hidden below may be able to advance our society, how we can entertain ourselves in the depths.

The earth beneath has provided humans with places to shelter, metals to make tools and weapons, power to feed machinery and the sanctuary to escape our own self-destruction. At the same time, forces under the Earth's surface have moved tectonic plates, causing earthquakes and volcanoes that have destroyed towns and cities. What lies beneath has both allowed civilisations to move forward and randomly checked our progress in unforgiving ways.

We know the immense potential that sits between us and the centre of the Earth's core, some 6,371km away, with a temperature approaching an unimaginable 6,000°C. And yet here we are in the 21st century, having barely scratched the surface of our underground world. The deepest point ever reached by humans on land is at the bottom of a gold mine in South Africa. That's a mere 4km down from the fresh air and daylight at ground level. It's less than 0.01% of the distance to the core.

Its intrigue fuelled by its inaccessibility, getting down into the bowels of the Earth has long fired the imagination of story-tellers. The Greeks passed down accounts of Hades, god of the Underworld, dwelling in the depths of the planet. The great French adventure novelist Jules Verne described a fantastical trip to the Earth's core through the Icelandic mountain Snæfell in *Journey to the Centre of the Earth*. The literary underground gauntlet was picked up by HG Wells at the end of the Victorian era, when he penned *The Time Machine*. Set thousands of years in the future, it depicts a new species, the Morlocks, who live underground and provide goods for the surface-dwelling Eloi and, in return, feed on their bodies. Meanwhile, in Wells's *The War of the Worlds*, the potential for starting a new life underground is explored by desperate victims of the Martians. Through the centuries, venturing down below has brought with it a sense of fear and adventure.

In the United Kingdom, digging deep has helped us to develop as a nation. Thousands of years ago, early Britons like Cheddar Man (whose remains were found in Gough's Cave in Cheddar Gorge) took shelter in natural caves to escape the elements and fierce predators. Tin miners in Cornwall traded

opposite Mysterious passageways and underground routes can be found all over Britain, including this tunnel looking out on Westminster.

opposite There are many ways to spend an enthralling day out in attractions beneath Britain, from castles and mines to bunkers and caverns.

with people working with copper ore in North Wales to create a new metal that could make pioneering tools and weapons, and that gave its name to their time period – the Bronze Age. Thousands sweated and toiled in mines to bring out the coal that powered the Industrial Revolution and the slate that still keeps the rain out of our houses. Whole communities have relied on the incomes paid to hard-working adults and children who disappeared into the darkness for shift after challenging shift.

When the dark years of World War II loomed over Europe, huge underground shelters in towns like Ramsgate, Stockport and Newcastle saved countless lives. Meanwhile, hidden passages in London, Dover and Liverpool allowed the war effort to be planned and executed without interruption. When the Cold War brought an icy chill to the continent, government strategists planning for a nuclear apocalypse again looked below ground for a solution. Bunkers in Essex and Fife contributed to a network of subterranean strongholds that, had it been necessary, would have attempted to maintain the rule of law and broadcast essential information to the nation.

Many of these places are no longer used, but instead an army of underground employees in the tourist industry now works below the surface to welcome you into these hidden depths that are so interlocked with the history of our nation. Many of them are unusual, some are bizarre and there are a few that are wonderfully eerie. Together, they provide the perfect solution for people wanting to try a different type of day out and an antidote to the conventional trips families tend to stick to on the surface. Visiting all 50 of the attractions in this book will take you on a fascinating journey of discovery through Britain's social and

An army of underground employees in the tourist industry now works below the surface to welcome you into these hidden depths that are so interlocked with the history of our nation.

INTRODUCTION

economic past, from early geological processes to the first settlers travelling across Doggerland; from the first miners honing raw materials to the incredible feats of engineering involved in developing transport and sewage systems; from hidden underground cables built to make the world metaphorically smaller to the hedonistic adventures of climbers in old slate mines. This enthralling collection of underground attractions is a rich resource for adventurous grown-ups and children alike; together, they convey the essence of British history and of the ordinary folk who spent years working in them.

I've thoroughly enjoyed my journey around Britain discovering places beneath the surface. There's a whole load of fun to be had down there. So get ready to go underground!

THE NORTH

EXPECT A GRITTY, INDUSTRIAL FEEL at many of Northern England's underground attractions. The National Coal Mining Museum and the coal seam at Beamish give a glimpse into the working lives of those toiling beneath the surface to power the factories and warm the homes of the 19th century. Tunnels through the Pennines and under the streets of Newcastle are examples of engineering achievements that made transporting raw materials easier and cost effective. And in the air raid shelters of Stockport and the planning bunker at Western Approaches, you'll see how northern determination overcame the threat posed by Hitler's Nazi Germany. Natural struggles on desolate terrain has also made a mark on what's beneath northern England. The band of limestone that stretches across the Yorkshire Dales has been eroded by surface water and underground streams over the centuries, allowing tourists to access the harsh and yet mesmerising subterranean landscapes that resulted. Being winched down into majestic Gaping Gill should be on the to-do-list of any outdoor adventurer, while beautiful formations are on display at the Ingleborough and White Scar Caves.

left The vast space beneath the Yorkshire Dales at Gaping Gill can be explored with the help of local caving clubs and is an unforgettable subterranean experience.

THE LOWDOWN

LOCATION Centre of Stockport, parking at Merseyway Shopping Centre

OPENING HOURS Closed Mon; Tues–Fri 1–5; Sat 10–5; Sun 11–5; bank hols 11–5
PRICE £5/£3.75

ADDRESS
61 Chestergate, Stockport, SK1 1NE
TEL 0161 474 1940

EMAIL airraid.shelters@stockport.gov.uk
WEBSITE www.stockport.gov.uk/topic/air-raid-shelters

01

STOCKPORT AIR RAID SHELTERS

A COMMUNITY REFUGE FROM THE BLITZ

Just how far these tunnels extend into the Stockport sandstone is impossible to determine from standing outside on the street. The frontage of these historically important shelters has a modern appearance, with nearby shops and taxi ranks giving the site a very urban feel. The hillside rises steeply behind the door to the shelters. A walkway winds upwards, buildings stand high above it and a bridge passes overhead. From here, the dug-out shelters pierce the hillside and form a grid system of subterranean passages and corners beneath the centre of Stockport.

Several small tunnels were discovered in 1938 and the initial plan was to use them for parking. But as war looked more and more likely, the plan was revised to extend them and create a public shelter for people in the town. Stockport Corporation sent out an engineer and the proposal to create air-raid shelters was soon given the go-ahead, albeit against the advice of the government. The sandstone may not have been the toughest rock to dig through, but the work was still challenging for those doing the job. A team of two men could make just over three feet of progress every day and faced a range of obstacles, including the weather. On cold days, their drills would freeze up, limiting the amount of tunnelling that could be done.

Before starting the tour of the shelters, you're given an audio guide. It doesn't look like the most hi-tech piece of kit, but it works remarkably well. As you guide yourself through the network of tunnels, you will see several signs marked 'Air Raid Precaution Shelter'. You simply have to hold your audio guide up to these circular yellow markers to trigger spoken information about the section you are in. After hearing the initial material, there'll be an option to select further information, allowing you to go into much more depth along the tour if you wish to do so. All the audio points are worth listening to, and there's a lot to be gained from taking the time to indulge in the extras.

Beyond the small shop, the first part of the tour involves standing in a reception area listening to early wartime radio clips. Neville Chamberlain's famous announcement at the start of the war is joined by several notable speeches by Winston

Largest purpose-built civilian air-raid shelters in the country

Sandstone tunnels designed to protect up to 4,000 Stockport residents from the Blitz

Nicknamed the Chestergate Hotel because it provided accommodation for so many

opposite Specialist rooms were allocated in the shelters, including areas for the all-important air raid warden and medical zones for emergency treatment.

below Life continued below ground while bombing was a threat.

right The town centre entrance conceals just how far these tunnels stretch into the northern sandstone.

Churchill. Local voices from Stockport also make an appearance. Historical recordings of people who lived back then reflect the mood within the town at the time as people waited for bombing raids and started to fear their impact. Some images appear on the ceiling during the presentation and then you're directed through a door leading into the tunnel network.

The red stone is incredibly atmospheric. Once you're inside these long tunnels it becomes easier to imagine what they would have been like filled with people. Different passages and small rooms heading off the main route were given specific purposes to maintain a sense of normality in these hidden halls. Perhaps most important of all were the rooms given over to tool storage. The digging and shovelling devices kept in them were to help people in the event of the tunnels collapsing, either from a natural accident or as the result of a bomb blast. The hope was that those stuck in here could dig their own way out to safety. Some other parts of this underground labyrinth were reserved for nursing mothers. Elsewhere, a large tunnel was designated as a medical area, complete with protected walls and concrete floors that were easier to clean. Ladies' and gents' toilets were provided, but as you might imagine, they were not very glamorous. Some of the loos were simply a seat cut into a large pipe. But the presence of toilets did mean that these shelters had adequate facilities to safely house people for an extended period of time. The electricity supply ensured that the shelters were also well lit throughout.

The Stockport Air Raid Shelters provide a rare opportunity to understand what people living in this northern town during World War II had to do when the sirens sounded. On hearing the eerie noise, workers from nearby shops, cinemas and offices were able to make their way to somewhere safe, underground. Daytime visits to the shelters are self-guiding, but there are evening trips given by experts that can be booked in advance. There is an additional charge for this, but you will be given a 90-minute guided tour covering fascinating local history and will encounter some tunnels which are not accessible to the public at other times.

GOING DEEPER...

War was declared on 1 September 1939, and many people expected the German bombing raids to begin immediately. But in the first year of World War II, most people in Greater Manchester did not experience any dramatic signs of being at war. Air-raid sirens were regularly tested in Stockport, but some locals didn't always appear to take them seriously because of the lack of German planes in the skies above. But when the Blitz hit London on 7 September 1940, people could see just how devastating the bombing raids were.

below The community did its best to keep spirits up.

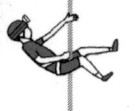

Three days before Christmas in 1940, Manchester bore the brunt of Hitler's Blitz. The city was attacked over a hellish 12-hour period. Nearly 300 German aircraft were involved in the Manchester raid on 22 December, dropping thousands of bombs and incendiary devices. The next day saw another air raid launched, this time coming during the night. These two devastating days of raids caused a huge amount of damage, killing 363 people and injuring over 1,000. Homelessness suddenly became a massive issue in the region, with 30,000 houses suffering damage and 5,000 people having no home to go back to.

Stockport had to deal with ten high-explosive bombs in the areas of Heaton Norris, Heaviley and Heaton Mersey, along with thousands of incendiaries that were unleashed with the intention of causing major fire damage. However, the people of the town were praised for the way they dealt with the incendiary bombs. With the aim of stopping fires from spreading, an information campaign in the build-up to the Blitz informed residents what to do if they saw one of these bombs. The actions of many Stockport people on the night of the Blitz stopped the destruction from being worse than it was. Despite their efforts, however, hundreds of houses throughout the town were damaged.

The manner in which people looked out for each other and took their responsibilities seriously helped to limit the loss of life. Getting to the shelter was a priority for local people if an air raid was threatened, so much so that the demand for places underground outstripped those available. Throughout 1940 and 1941, work was carried out to extend the shelters, meaning that as many as 6,500 people could seek sanctuary in the red sandstone tunnels.

The town centre shelters were still used throughout the year following the Blitz by hundreds of people wanting safety in case another bombing raid was launched.

After the Manchester Blitz in 1940, there were few further air raids that hit Stockport. The town centre shelters, though, were still used throughout the following year by hundreds of people wanting safety in case another bombing raid was launched. When it became apparent that Stockport was unlikely to be targeted again, the number of people sheltering in the tunnels dropped. By the end of 1942, there were only 50 people regularly using the shelter. The decision was made to close the shelters in 1943, though it would have been possible to open them again in an emergency. After the war, the closure became permanent and they remained off limits until they were reopened for public visits in 1996.

02

THE BEATLES STORY

A MAGICAL MYSTERY TOUR

Since John Lennon met Paul McCartney at a village fete in the summer of 1957, lots of changes have been seen at Liverpool's Albert Dock. It was once a thriving industrial hub at the heart of the city, but industrial decline and mass unemployment ripped the northern soul out of the dock during the 1970s and 1980s. Today, though, after years of reinvestment, the Albert Dock area at the side of the river Mersey is once more a thriving part of this great city's economy. The jobs today come from coffee shops, restaurants, art galleries and museums rather than from ships arriving from afar. It's good to see these historic buildings teeming with life once more, and The Beatles Story is at the centre of it all.

Occupying the Britannia Vaults in the basement of the dock building, Liverpool's world-class Beatles attraction provides a link between the city's industrial past and the musical history it's well known for. Leave the posh eateries at street level and descend the stairs to embark on an underground magical mystery tour about Liverpool's most famous sons. Getting tickets online beforehand could save you having to queue at

Tells the story of the Fab Four, from their formation to post-Beatles life

Audio guides and videos, along with much memorabilia, bring the band's story to life

Contains a recreated version of the Cavern, where the Beatles played nearly 300 gigs

the door and could secure the all-important audio guide around your neck a little faster. The experience benefits so much from the electronic guide, which not only has a wide range of spoken information but also shows pictures and plays a selection of videos. It plays a pivotal role in introducing the story of the Beatles to you, starting with the school days of the original four – John Lennon, Paul McCartney, George Harrison and Pete Best, who was famously replaced by Ringo Starr. But don't rely on the headphones entirely for this visit. There are so many other things to see and listen to, and you'll want to discuss them with other people in your group. There's far too much happening here to warrant going around in silence.

The Beatles Story is told in chronological order, and recounts how a chance meeting brought together one of the world's hottest songwriting partnership, Lennon and McCartney. Rooms re-create their early days playing in Liverpool's Casbah and the clubs of Hamburg. The influence of Brian Epstein is then examined before you come to one of the key elements of the story – the Cavern Club. The room you now find yourself in is a great replica of that famous club, right down to the band names inscribed on the wall and the neatly positioned chairs. From there, the route heads to the recording studio, where visitors hear from George Martin as Ringo Starr picks up the drumsticks. We're then indulged with stories about the band's albums. Photo opportunities are available in a yellow submarine and in front of a huge version of the *Sgt. Pepper's Lonely Hearts Club Band* album cover. Beatlemania in America is another high point of the story, and you can sit in aircraft seats listening to accounts of their arrival in the United States.

Save plenty of time for the large room at the end of the story, when the post-1970 careers of the Beatles are put centre stage. Their achievements are relayed through displays, music and videos. Each of the Fab Four have their own seated area where you can relax and indulge in McCartney belting out 'Live and Let Die', Lennon's political protests, Harrison's wonderful 'My Sweet Lord' and Starr narrating *Thomas the Tank Engine*. Solo career moments you may have forgotten about are also explored here, including Ringo Starr's movie appearance in *The Magic Christian* and Paul McCartney's film, *Give My Regards to Broad Street*.

previous page
Liverpool's Cavern Club is synonymous with the early days of the Beatles.

At the end of The Beatles Story, the Fab4 Café is a great place to reflect on what you've just seen and maybe enjoy a Beatles-themed bun with a drink. Large murals on the wall remind you exactly where you are. Before you exit to street level, the Fab4 Store has a huge range of souvenirs, from T-shirts and Christmas decorations to bags and bears.

Your own personal Beatles story can continue above ground after your visit. A walk down towards the Royal Liver Building brings you to a stunning statue of the Beatles that is a selfie hotspot. The Cavern Club also puts on two-hour coach tours of the city, calling at significant places such as Penny Lane and Strawberry Fields before bringing you back to enjoy music at the famous venue. And if you're in town on a Thursday night, check out the Beatles tribute band at the Cavern if you really want to step back in time.

GOING DEEPER...

The Beatles Story is the world's largest permanent exhibition devoted to the life and times of the band. Since it opened in May 1990, over 4 million people have visited from 100 different countries. It's an attraction that has won several awards and now pulls in 300,000 visitors a year. And it's incredibly fitting

below The Beatles Story is home to memorabilia linked to the story of the Fab Four.

that this homage to the Beatles is situated in their hometown of Liverpool, which will forever be linked with Beatlemania. The location of the story is also significant on the world stage. The Albert Dock is part of the Liverpool Maritime Mercantile City UNESCO World Heritage Site. Containing the largest concentration of Grade I listed buildings anywhere in the country, the riverside setting is the most visited multiple-use attraction outside London and has played a key part in reinvigorating Liverpool.

Work on constructing the historic dock started in 1841. It took five years to build the site that covered 1.25 million square feet, and which was officially opened by Prince Albert on 30 July 1846. It was the first structure in the country to be constructed entirely from iron, brick and stone. This was highly significant because the wooden warehouses that preceded it were at a significant risk of being damaged by fire. Two years after it opened, the Albert Dock became the first dock to install hydraulic hoists and proudly boasted that it could accommodate sailing ships of up to 1,000 tonnes.

But the glory days of the dock were short-lived. By the time the Victorian era came to a close, only 7% of the vessels arriving in Liverpool were the sailing ships suited to the Albert Dock. Thanks to the changing nature of global shipping, the pioneering developments at Albert Dock were destined for the history books a mere half a century after they were leading the world. Following its closure in 1972, the famous buildings fell into disrepair and the dock silted up.

below The international appeal of John, Paul, George and Ringo is still phenomenally strong.

As happened in many other northern cities that experienced the crippling effects of industrial decline, attention in Liverpool turned to regeneration in the 1980s. Projects designed to breathe new life into the dock area kicked off in 1983. Five years later, the Albert Dock as we know it today was opened by Prince Charles and went on to win several awards. Aside from The Beatles Story it's also home to a number of other popular tourist attractions, including Tate Liverpool, the Merseyside Maritime Museum and the International Slavery Museum.

LOCATION	OPENING HOURS	ADDRESS 1–3 Rumford	EMAIL info@western	THE LOWDOWN
Liverpool	10–5: closed Weds	Street, Exchange Flags,	approaches.org.uk	
centre, behind	PRICE £10.50/£9,	Liverpool, L2 8SZ	WEBSITE www.western	
Town Hall	family £30	TEL 0151 227 2008	approaches.org.uk	

FIGHTING THE BATTLE OF THE ATLANTIC

03 WESTERN APPROACHES

Glance up to the sky from the Western Approaches building and you'll pick out the famous Royal Liver Building, opened in 1911 and sporting the two fabled liver birds on top. There can be no doubt that you're in Liverpool, where redeveloped docks just a stone's throw away allow you to enjoy art, shopping and coffee. The docks have always been hugely important to this great northern city, and at their height they dominated the local economy. But during World War II, the dock area of Liverpool took on a different role, one which was vitally important for the nation's survival. The port of Liverpool saw a huge amount of supplies arrive from America via the Atlantic, along with many US soldiers. Without this essential supply being maintained, the war may have had a very different outcome. The fact that it was maintained was due in no small part to the work of a dedicated team that was beavering away beneath Liverpool's Rumford Street to keep track of the much-feared German U-boats on their deadly Atlantic patrols.

Everything to see at the Western Approaches is below street level, so you head down a slope and negotiate some stairs

21

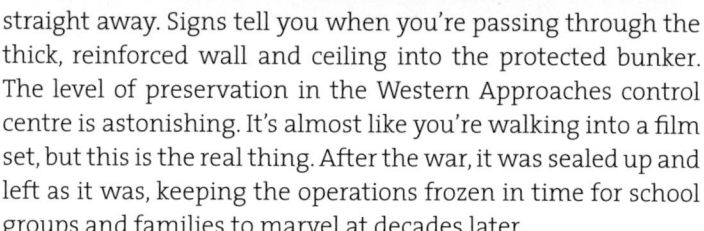

NAVAL TELEPRINTER STATION

above Western Approaches appeals to history buffs because of the many pieces of original equipment on display.

previous page Western Approaches allows visitors to walk around historic rooms where the pivotal Battle of the Atlantic was orchestrated during WWII.

straight away. Signs tell you when you're passing through the thick, reinforced wall and ceiling into the protected bunker. The level of preservation in the Western Approaches control centre is astonishing. It's almost like you're walking into a film set, but this is the real thing. After the war, it was sealed up and left as it was, keeping the operations frozen in time for school groups and families to marvel at decades later.

The entire monitoring operation at Western Approaches was dependent on radio transmissions passing sensitive information in and out, and these transmissions were driven by electricity, so some of the first things to look at in this bunker are associated with the power supply. Liverpool was one of the worst-hit cities during the German bombing raids, and the city's electricity source was not always guaranteed. The planners of this bunker therefore made it a priority to provide a back-up generator and, with a huge amount of irony, used a diesel-powered engine seized from a German U-boat for this purpose.

There are plenty of maps displayed on this self-guided tour, from small paper versions in private offices to a huge plan of Europe and the Atlantic on the wall of the operations room. Maps were at the heart of everything that happened here, as the dedicated staff were tasked with keeping an eye on what was happening out at sea. Young women with a talent for mathematics were employed to take down and plot hundreds of coordinates in a real-life game of Battleships where secret messages informed the moves and countermoves. The map you see on the wall is particularly useful at highlighting the strategic nature of this nautical cat-and-mouse challenge.

Suspected sightings of U-boats saw a white symbol placed on the map. A black version meant the location was confirmed. The information gathered within this Liverpudlian bunker could be the difference between life and death for those making hazardous sea journeys hundreds of miles away.

A World War II bunker that monitored the battle taking place in the Atlantic Ocean

Containing 100 rooms, the secret underground facility was bomb and gas proof

The U-boat menace in the Atlantic was the feature of the war that most frightened Winston Churchill

Visitors today are free to wander around the Western Approaches HQ at their leisure, reading the many information boards to get a better idea of what life was like beneath war-torn Liverpool. Access was not always as straightforward, though. Signs posted on doors show that entrance to many areas was restricted back when the bunker was in active use, while other painted instructions insist on 'silence'. During the war there was not just a single checkpoint where identification papers were verified – there were several placed all over the building. This allowed closer control of the movement of staff and, crucially, control of who was going in and out of the operations room. The key cupboard was strictly monitored, and guards took their role very seriously. The whole aim of security at Western Approaches was to make sure classified information remained secret. Staff at the time knew how data collected in these underground passages could affect thousands of lives out at sea and influence the fate of millions on land.

below Security was extremely important at Western Approaches; guards stationed here kept a watchful eye on every person coming in and out of the Main Operations Room.

placing ...ent their gh to the next point. The particularly important as it kept watch over anyone entering or leaving the Main Operations Room.

The high importance of what was going on at Western Approaches meant increased security, to ensure that the intelligence known in the bunker remained secret and in the right hands.

At this checkpoint, guards would have been stationed for long hours and kept watch over the key cabinet, on the inside of which can be seen a pin-up poster, perhaps placed there on a particularly gruelling shift.

03 WESTERN APPROACHES

GOING DEEPER...

The Battle of the Atlantic is not as well known as some other key World War II campaigns, such as the Battle of Britain, the Dunkirk evacuation and the D-Day landings. But the war which raged across the whole of this vast ocean was hugely significant and influenced the direction of the war. It was a fierce tactical battle and the only one which lasted from the first day of the war until the last. Prime Minister Winston Churchill said the battle in the Atlantic was the single aspect of World War II which truly frightened him. He knew that success depended on getting vital supplies into the country, and it was these sources of help that the German U-boats were targeting. As an island nation, Britain required more than one million tonnes of imported goods every week to enable it to survive and fight on. Most of this came from North America in large convoys of ships manned by sailors who were all too aware of the dangers hidden below the ocean.

Monitoring the U-boats and relaying their position to supply ships was the job of those working under the streets of Liverpool. Sightings of the terrifying Nazi vessels – both confirmed and suspected – were plotted on large wall maps in the hope of providing Allies with safe passage. There were many successes during the Battle of the Atlantic, thanks to aerial monitoring by the Royal Air Force and the interception of German transmissions by the Enigma code breakers. But the campaign took a heavy toll throughout the entire length of the war. Hardly a day went by without the loss of a merchant ship and crew. Many Allied and British merchant seamen were taken as prisoners of war during the conflict at sea. By the end of World War II, 2,603 merchant ships had been sunk, along with 175 naval vessels. Losses on the German side were also great, with 783 U-boats being destroyed. A huge number of men lost their lives at sea during the campaign, including over 6,000 Royal Navy sailors and more than 30,000 merchant seamen. Even though they were civilians – and as a result were thought of unfavourably by some because they did not wear a uniform – it was these sailors who often found themselves thrust to the front line of one of the war's most terrifying battles. In addition to the U-boats, they also had to endure the threats from aerial attack and from mines in the ocean. The natural dangers of the sea were also a concern, especially for crews sailing on the many ships that were not seaworthy.

> Monitoring the U-boats and relaying their position to supply ships was the job of those working under the streets of Liverpool.

04

STANDEDGE TUNNEL

A TUNNEL THROUGH THE MIGHTY PENNINES

Use the free car park at Marsden train station or arrive by rail and you'll enjoy the most charming approach to the longest, deepest and highest canal tunnel in the country. This 15-minute stroll by the water gives you time to take in the canal-side setting, and it's a very peaceful route. You'll get to see familiar sights of canal life, including the occasional duck, tranquil water scenes and people stretching their legs along the towpath. But as you round the corner and approach the Standedge Visitor Centre, it's time to abandon everything you thought you knew about canals cutting through the countryside.

Many engineers in the late 18th century were obsessed with canals, which were the new form of transport. They were faster than the packhorses they replaced, and there was money to be made in these pioneering water channels. Textile mills in this part of the world needed coal and wool transporting regularly and efficiently, and canals were the modern way of moving raw materials. A minor obstacle like the Pennine Hills wasn't going to stop determined engineers and industrialists,

Britain's longest canal tunnel, as well as its deepest (because of the mass of rock sitting above the water) and highest (due to its lofty position in the Peak District).

Played an important role in northern England's Industrial Revolution

Take a 30-minute boat ride into the tunnel or opt for a two-hour journey right through to the other side

so in 1794 they began hammering and blasting their way through to create a 3.1-mile tunnel.

When you first see Standedge Tunnel, it looks tiny – a small hole burrowing into a large hill. From a distance it doesn't seem like a boat can fit through it. As you get closer, your sense of perspective changes and you come to fully appreciate the sheer scale of achievement that allows boats to be swallowed in the tunnel's darkness and lets them emerge, two hours later, on the other side of the Pennines. It's a monumental journey, and the distance covered makes this the longest canal tunnel in the country. There are two types of boat trip you can enjoy inside the tunnel. If you're pushed for time, a 30-minute taster will take you a few hundred metres inside to give you a feel for what it's like before reversing back out. Those wanting a more substantial day out may like to go the whole hog and experience the full two-hour journey right through to the other side. The return trip is usually arranged with a local taxi firm. Special overground walking tours are also available along the old packhorse route, with National Trust experts on hand to safely return you to Standedge and fill you in on the rich history along the way. Whichever you opt for, the voyage through the tunnel is one you won't forget. Book ahead and pick up your tickets in the café.

Once you get onto the boat, there are forward-facing seats inside for those wanting to enjoy the journey under a clear Perspex roof. But look for the open-air seats at the front and back of the boat for the best experience. Here, you'll need to wear a hard hat and cope with the occasional drop of water from the roof of the tunnel, but you'll get a much better feel for what the tunnel is like.

The guide taking you on the journey will be able to answer any questions about the history of the tunnel, its restoration and modern-day uses as well as pointing out interesting features along the way. These include variations in the brick-work that reflect different building methods, small channels leading to the adjoining railway tunnels, areas where the local bedrock provides a natural roof to the tunnel and distance markers for the 'leggers' who used to move the boats along the canal using their feet.

previous page Boat owners tackling the full length of Standedge Tunnel need an expert on board to help out.

Halfway through the tour it's time for lights out. Revealing just how dark it is in this subterranean passage makes it clear how deep you are under the Pennine Hills. Experiencing the darkness on this underground boat trip also gives you some idea of the conditions those early tunnellers worked in. Candles provided the only light, making this engineering feat even more remarkable.

GOING DEEPER...

At the time it was built, this was the most expensive tunnel ever constructed, costing nearly £124,000. The work was authorised by an Act of Parliament in 1794, and the engineer chosen to oversee the project was Benjamin Outram, a man well known for his work on canals elsewhere in the country. Constructing a 5,000-metre-long trans-Pennine passage underneath up to

left In the heart of the Pennines, Standedge Tunnel's entrance occupies a picture postcard position.

194m of land was always going to be a challenging task, but Outram reckoned it would be a fairly straightforward affair because of the nature of the relatively soft gritstone rock. Sadly, he was wrong. The project was riddled with difficulties. It was originally predicted to take five years, but it wasn't officially opened until 17 years after tunnelling started.

Problems encountered during the tunnelling work included continual difficulties in finding contractors who were willing to carry out the work in dark and difficult conditions. There was also far more water seeping into the tunnel than was first thought. Outram himself left the project in 1801 because of the lack of progress being made, and the managers had to return to Parliament to raise more funds. Tunnelling was under way at each side of the Pennines, and the two ends finally met each other deep underground in 1809. Two years later, the grand opening was held.

The new trans-Pennine route was immediately popular, with up to 40 boats a day making the trip through the tunnel.

below Early journeys were propelled by workers pushing legs against the tunnel roof.

The number of boats allowed through each day was restricted partly because of the time it took them to make their way through its full length, and partly because of the tunnel's very narrow width: there are no passing places and a one-way system is used.

The popularity of this engineering wonder was ultimately short-lived, thanks in part to the coming of the railways in the Victorian era, and then to the development of road networks in the 20th century. Canals were no longer viewed as the speedy option they once were. The last commercial boat to use the Standedge Canal Tunnel did so in 1921, and in 1944 it was abandoned entirely, soon falling into disrepair.

A campaign to restore the tunnel started to gain momentum in the 1990s, and funds totalling £5 million were allocated to opening Standedge Tunnel up once more. Essential maintenance was carried out on the walls of the tunnel and much of the waterway was dredged. The grand reopening in 2001 saw a boat pass through the tunnel once again. Today, private boats are allowed to use the tunnel and many canal-users have the route prioritised on their tick-list. But if you're planning on bringing your boat here, you must book a slot in advance to travel into the tunnel. On days when access is allowed, only three boats are permitted to travel in each direction. And every boat owner must arrange to have a chaperone from the Canal and Rivers Trust to ensure a safe passage.

05
NATIONAL COAL MINING MUSEUM FOR ENGLAND

A MINE WITH A HUMAN HEART

Approaching the National Coal Mining Museum, it's hard to imagine that only a couple of decades ago much of the land in these parts was being mined and that many of the villages were completely dependent on jobs under the ground. Today, the coal fields of Yorkshire have been regenerated, with varying degrees of success, into housing estates, country parks, nature reserves and shopping centres. Caphouse Colliery may have produced its last coal in the 1980s, but the legacy of the mine lives on thanks to this quaint and charming museum. At the heart of its success are the former miners who still make their daily journey down to the coal face. Rather than blasting coal from the bowels of the earth, however, they now descend the 140m into the ground to guide tourists around the notoriously difficult working conditions. The humour and camaraderie shared between these guides – all decked out in their orange coal-mining gear, complete with

THE LOWDOWN

LOCATION West of Overton on the A642

OPENING HOURS Daily 10–5
PRICE Free admission to museum. Underground tours £3

ADDRESS Caphouse Colliery, New Road, Overton, Wakefield, WF4 4RH

TEL 01924 848806
EMAIL info@ncm.org.uk
WEBSITE www.ncm.org.uk

hard hat and lamp light – is the really price-less quality of the tour here. It's a friendly journey underground, made heart-warming and genuine because these people are the real deal.

Tours to the coal face can be booked in advance, but most people sign up for the trip when they arrive. Head to the museum's shop and you'll be allocated a time. There can be up to 31 trips organised on busy days, so you're unlikely to have to wait a long time. If you have 30–45 minutes to wait, now's the time to wander around the museum's exhibits and soak in the area's mining history. You'll find out about the origins of mining at Caphouse and the highs and lows of the industry through the years. The exhibition keeps returning to the theme of social struggle, which has gone hand in hand with mining over the centuries.

Ten minutes before your tour time, follow in the path of real miners as you queue up for your lamp light and hard hat. Hand in contraband items that increase the risk of explosions (lighters, phones, cameras, car keys – basically, anything with a battery) so that they can be locked up until you return to the surface. Then it's time to make your way to the cage – the

opposite Former coal miners with years of pit experience lead the tours.

left The once familiar sight of a winding wheel still greets visitors at the museum.

![Machinery photograph]

above Machinery spanning over a century is on display, showing how coal mining methods have developed.

lift that will take you all the way down. And it is literally a cage. A rattling, juddering cage that used to carry 27 miners down to the coal – and sometimes more on the way back up as workers hurried to leave when their shift finished. Just outside, watch out for a double-decker cage that was used to transport even more miners up and down the lift shaft. You may well feel like a sardine yourself as you squeeze in to begin the journey down to the all-important raw material that was the driving force behind the Industrial Revolution – coal. (The claustrophobic or nervous may want to know at this stage that there is an emergency exit you can walk to in the unlikely event of the winding wheel malfunctioning.)

Difficult working conditions and incredibly large, powerful machinery await you at the bottom. Once again, the greatest asset here is your tour guide. The guides have all spent years down the pit, know the job inside out and welcome your questions about life under the ground. They'll also tell you about how tough life was during the strike in the 1980s, the terrible accidents that took place and, of course, the difficulties faced by entire communities when the industry was mothballed by Tory governments under Margaret Thatcher and John Major.

On your return to the surface via the draughty tunnel shaft you can head to the shop. But the workers of yesteryear would have headed straight for the showers, knowing that the first ones up got the warmest water. The teamwork and strong sense of community is best summed up by an old mining saying: *Underground, they watched each other's backs. On the surface, they washed each other's backs.*

GOING DEEPER...

Mining at Caphouse Colliery – named after a nearby building called Cap House – dates back to 1778, when James Milne leased two coal seams. Mining had been carried out in the area for at least 200 years before this, but Milne oversaw the excavation of shafts down to the Flockton Thick Seam (found on a 1791 plan of mining operations). Health and safety was not a major concern in those days, and the only protection from the deep shafts was a simple wooden fence. After the new road (now the A642) was built right by the side of the site, Sir John Lister-Kay took over the lease and the shafts were deepened by 15m. The Victorian era saw some coal seams exhausted, new shafts sunk to access nearby seams and other shafts sunk even deeper. The railway offered a new means of transporting coal from the site, and in 1854 Caphouse Colliery was linked to the main line. Advances in technology saw more and more coal extracted from Caphouse, and by the end of the 1970s there were a phenomenal 250,000 tonnes of coal leaving it every year.

The idea of setting up a mining museum in the Wakefield area had been talked about for some time in the early 1980s. Nearby Walton Colliery was also an initial contender to house the museum, but Caphouse won the day because of the range of buildings on the surface and the steam winder linked to the No. 1 shaft. Work started on converting Caphouse Colliery into a museum in 1986, and the grand opening came two years later. The successful application for 'national status' in 1995 broadened the museum's appeal and saw it becoming the home of the British Coal Collection of mining machinery.

below Young children used to work in the mine, but thankfully today's junior visitors don't break into a sweat.

THE LOWDOWN

LOCATION Short walk from Clapham village. North of Settle off the A65,

OPENING HOURS Feb half term to end of Oct daily 10–4 (open to 5 during school holidays). Open three weekends before Christmas

PRICE £9/£7.50/ £4.50 family £25
ADDRESS Ingleborough Cave, Clapham, LA2 8EE

TEL 01524 251242
EMAIL info@ingle boroughcave.co.uk
WEBSITE www.ingle boroughcave.co.uk

06

INGLEBOROUGH CAVE

A TREASURE TROVE OF NATURAL WONDER

The small village of Clapham has more than its fair share of underground features. Ingleborough Cave welcomes visitors for most of the year, and a little further up the path, Gaping Gill is a popular attraction for the two weeks it is accessible to the public. Both are accessed by the nature trail leading away from the centre of the village. It's well signed and you'll need some change to pay the toll as the path begins.

Initially the path is a little steep, but it soon levels out and you can enjoy the surrounding countryside and small reservoir on the way up to the cave. It takes about half an hour to reach and the path is well maintained all the way. When you arrive at Ingleborough Cave, register for the next available tour inside the small reception building in front of the limestone cliff. The trips into the cave's passageways take place every half hour or so, meaning there could be a short wait. But if the weather is fine, spending a little time relaxing before your tour can be inspiring. It's a picture-postcard type of place, with a beautiful limestone bridge, a small stream flowing beneath it and steep hills rising either side of the valley. It is here that the river emerges from underneath the cliff after spending a short stretch of its journey below ground, during which it passed through Gaping Gill. Although it was once a tight squeeze to get into the cave, today it's accessed through a door that has been built into the entrance. There's an area outside where the tour group gathers and where the guide will run through some health and safety precautions. Then it's hard hats on and into the cave.

The initial part of Ingleborough Cave was excavated by the Victorian cave enthusiasts who first discovered this entrance to what is a very comprehensive network of passages. Their initial exploration wasn't as extensive as that undertaken on the tour today because back then the route into the hillside was blocked after only a few metres by a solid wall of rock. When the landowner cleverly monitored the cave following a heavy flood, he realised there were underground stores of water lying behind this rock wall. And so a decision was made to find out what lay in the space beyond. A supply of explosives was used to blast away the rock that was preventing further exploration: this was Victorian England, of course, when less respect was often given to natural features.

opposite Lighting helps to bring out the cave's beauty.

below Flowstone creates many strange-looking features.

The explosions smashed open the rock and the water came pouring out, allowing more excavation of the cave system to take place. The opening up of these previously hidden parts of Ingleborough Cave allowed Victorian visitors to see the underground wonders beneath the Yorkshire Dales for the first time, and tourists are still awestruck by them today. The main difference between then and now is that today there is lighting; you will get to see the features more clearly with the help of lights that really bring out their beauty. The initial explorers would have gained only a fraction of this

06 INGLEBOROUGH CAVE

insight with their candles. Apart from the lighting, though, the natural features are largely unchanged from the 19th century. The stalagmites and other limestone creations are developing at such extremely slow rates that you see them pretty much as they were in Queen Victoria's day.

Look out for remains of the two underground reservoirs during the first part of the tour, the lines on the wall showing where the water used to reach. Beyond, there are treasures to be seen at every turn as the cave system unfolds into a wonderland of flowstone, stalagmites, stalactites and pillars. With a stream running at the side of the path virtually all the way, the cave is wet and there are many pools to see along the way. Sometimes the lights in the cave catch these still pools of crystal clear water to produce staggering reflections. Many look fantastically deep when in fact there is only a few millimetres of water between the surface and the bottom. Others reflect stalactite features to create illusions of Atlantis-style cities under the water. On the way out, there is a pool with hundreds of coins at the bottom, thrown in over the decades by hopeful visitors making a wish. Many have been worn away over the years as they have lain in their watery resting place.

> Still pools of crystal clear water reflect stalactite features to create illusions of Atlantis-style cities under the water.

GOING DEEPER...

The depths of the cave system beyond the entrance to Ingleborough Cave are still being explored and continue to reveal new secrets, nearly 200 years after their initial discovery. When those curious Victorians first took a look inside Ingleborough Cave and then blasted their way further into the hillside, they could only imagine what they would find. We now know that the underground system of passages from this show cave leads up to Gaping Gill and forms part of a world-famous 17km underground network. Discovery and exploration has been a slow affair beneath Ingleborough, one of the hills making up Yorkshire's Three Peaks circuit that's hugely popular with walkers. The dark, dangerous conditions and the need for diving equipment have ensured that those looking for new subterranean routes over the last two centuries have not found the task easy. After the initial visit inside Ingleborough Cave in 1837, it was to be another 58 years before the celebrated French speleologist Édouard-Alfred Martel made the first descent of Gaping Gill. Using rope ladders and candles, Martel was able to

stand at the bottom of Gaping Gill's hidden waterfall and gaze upwards from the bottom of the cave in 1895. As the decades passed, it was believed but not proved that the water in Gaping Gill flowed beneath the Yorkshire Dales to Ingleborough Cave. It was not until 1983 that the journey along this link between the two caves was completed by humans. A team of cavers from Bradford Potholing Club together with experienced cave divers successfully negotiated flooded areas of the cave network known as sumps. Using breathing apparatus, they made their way along dry passages and through deep water to finally chart the route between Ingleborough Cave and Gaping Gill. Although the potholes leading to this cave system should only be tackled by people with the relevant experience and expertise, those with the know-how are still making important discoveries here. As recently as 2001, the remains of a woolly rhinoceros were found a short way beyond the point where the public tour ends. The full extent of the wonders of Ingleborough Cave have yet to be revealed.

below The full extent of the cave's treasures is still being uncovered.

THE LOWDOWN

LOCATION Head northeast out of Ingleton on the B6255	OPENING HOURS Feb–Oct daily from 10, Nov–Jan weekends from 10.	PRICE £10.35/ £6.75, family £28.60	ADDRESS Ingleton, North Yorks, LA6 3AW
			TEL 015242 41244
			EMAIL info@whitescarcave.co.uk
			WEBSITE www.whitescarcave.co.uk

07

WHITE SCAR CAVE

AN UNDERGROUND WATERFALL BENEATH THE DALES

Hidden deep inside northern England's hills, this natural wonder occupies what can be a very blustery position in the heart of the Yorkshire Dales National Park. On the remote road leading out of quaint Ingleton towards the dramatic Ribblehead Viaduct and the cheese-making village of Hawes, the White Scar Cave building cuts a lonely figure in the countryside. It's hard to miss. As well as a brown sign luring you in, the building has 'CAVES' written in large white letters across the roof.

Visit in fine weather and you'll see the sun beating down on the green, rolling hills that are home to the sheep farms and dry-stone walls the Dales are famous for. If the elements are not on your side, you'll be battered by wind and driving rain as soon as you leave your car. The weather here can be unforgiving. But don't get too downhearted – a run of wet days can give this trip a serious edge. The expert-led tour follows the route of an underground stream and visits a subterranean waterfall, and the sights and sounds are heightened if there has been some wet weather. (Note, however, that too much rain in this notoriously change-able Yorkshire microclimate can cause the White Scar Cave to close for health and safety reasons; the passageways can become impassable and very dangerous.) Whatever the weather, expect the ground to be wet and be prepared for constant drips from the roof. Visitors journey along a river channel far below Ingleborough – one of the hills forming York-shire's Three Peaks walk – and a few splashes are par for the course.

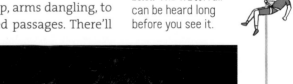

The longest show cave in Britain

Dramatic underground waterfall discovered in the 1920s

Beautiful stalactites nicknamed carrots amid a range of subterranean formations

The ticket booth opens a few minutes before each tour is due to begin. Journeys underground leave regularly, but any time waiting can be spent grabbing a cuppa in the café and browsing around the small shop. Once you've bought your ticket, you'll be kitted out with a hard hat – and if you're on the tall side, you're going to need it. There are two fairly lengthy sections on the cave tour where most people will need to stoop. The guides call one of them the 'Gorilla Walk' because of the primate pose visitors take when they stoop, arms dangling, to make their way through the low, cramped passages. There'll probably also be some folk making gorilla-like noises when their hard hat connects with the rock and catches them off guard.

opposite The stunning roof of the cave, thousands of years in the making.

below The waterfall can be heard long before you see it.

The walk through the under-ground river channel is mesmer-ising. You'll find yourself staring at swirling patterns in the rock that have been etched by thou-sands of years' erosion. There are astonishing stalactites, stalagmites and curious shapes formed of flowstone (a calcium carbonate layer deposited by thin sheets of flowing water). Some of these – look out for the Devil's Tongue and Arum Lily – are fantastically beautiful and look like they have been sculpted by an artist. The fossilised coral reef and sea creatures that your tour guide will point out are

07 WHITE SCAR CAVE

even more bewildering, and act as a reminder that this part of the world was once at the Equator and home to tropical seas teeming with life.

After climbing a series of steps, you arrive at Battlefield Cavern, so named by a caver who discovered it in 1971 and concluded that the boulder-strewn floor resembled a battle-field from the Great War. The enormity of the cavern – the longest you'll get to see in this country – is staggering. It is an impressive 1,600 metres in length – that's four laps of London's 2012 Olympic running track. This huge space was once filled to the top with water, which eventually drained out, resulting in some of the ceiling collapsing at the same time. This is the reason so many large rocks are littering the floor. The highlight of your time in the Battlefield Cavern will be when the lights are turned off – which is not as scary as it sounds. An ultra-violet beam is shone onto the ceiling, revealing the unforget-table sight of hundreds of glowing straw stalactites, all slowly extending down at the rate of 1cm every 200 years.

The same route in reverse takes you back to the entrance, and though it is taken a lot quicker this time, and without commentary from your tour guide, there is still plenty to look at. Take care to look out for strange shapes in the rock you may have missed earlier. But most of all, savour the sound of the thundering river flowing deep beneath the Yorkshire land-scape. You can hear the waterfall as soon as you enter the cave, but nothing really prepares you for rounding a corner and seeing it cascading from nowhere into a plunge pool that wouldn't look out of place on a tropical island.

GOING DEEPER...

When Christopher Long came to the Yorkshire Dales on holiday in 1923 and saw water flowing out of the hillside, he was intrigued and decided to investigate further. Crawling into the low, cramped passage, Long heard the distant roar of water and slowly edged his way towards the waterfall you see on your visit.

While your stroll to the waterfall takes a few minutes through a purposely dug tunnel, spare a thought for the deter-mination Christopher Long showed. His trip took two hours as he struggled into the hillside, wearing just his jumper, shorts and walking boots. His way was lit only by a bowler hat that had four candles propped up around the edge. His lust for exploration was quite remarkable. Not many others would

opposite When the main lights go off, ultra violet beams highlight thousands of years of stalactite formation.

above Eroded by water, the underground caverns are vast, cathedral-like spaces.

have the nerve and grit to crawl through a dark underground passageway in pursuit of a noise.

Long returned to the caves and discovered subterranean lakes, which he swam across, and he intended to open the underground passages to visitors. Sadly, though, he suffered from depression and in 1924 he took his own life. The caves were nevertheless eventually opened and the first manager, Tom Greenwood, found many extra passages during the 1930s.

Following the discovery of the Battlefield Cavern in 1971, discussions took place about how this enormous space could also be opened to the public. It wasn't until 1991 that visitors could stand in the cavern, following a project involving Cornish tin miners digging a 65m tunnel and the installation of an additional 400m of paths.

There are many natural processes taking place in the White Scar Cave that have led to the underground landscape you can see today. Some of the most important involve the limestone rock being worn away. This happens because of the erosive power of flowing water, but also because natural acid in the groundwater dissolves the limestone. Chemical reactions in the water lead to calcite deposits, most famously seen in the hollow straw stalactites that grow down from the roof of the cave. Fast-dripping water leaves rings of calcite behind, creating the tube-like stalactites that can be seen in the Battlefield Cavern. These processes are still taking place, meaning that visitors to the cave fifty years from now will have an ever-so-slightly different view from those who go there today. More significant changes in these amazing spaces beneath the Yorkshire Dales, though, will take thousands of years.

THE LOWDOWN

LOCATION
Ingleborough hillside 90-min walk from Clapham village, (on the A65 north of Settle).

OPENING HOURS Members of the public can be winched down during two weeks of the year when caving clubs organise a meet. This is usually at the end of May with Bradford Pothole Club and in the middle of August with Craven Pothole Club.

PRICE £15 (over 7s only)
CONTACT DETAILS CRAVEN POTHOLE CLUB Email: secretary@craven potholeclub.org; BRADFORD POT-HOLE CLUB Tel: 01274 710298
WEBSITES www.cravenpothole club.org; www.bpc-cave.org.uk

08 GAPING GILL

WINCHED DOWN INTO THE ABYSS

Gaping Gill is far too dangerous for members of the public to explore on their own. It's the territory of potholing and caving experts. Fortunately, however, two local potholing clubs organise cave meets at Gaping Gill every year so that inexperienced folk can be safely winched down to see its immense beauty. The Bradford Potholing Club spend a week on Ingleborough at the end of May, while in the second half of August it's the turn of the Craven Potholing Club. For the rest of the year, Gaping Gill is fenced off, with warning signs posted nearby. So, the first thing you need to do when planning this fabulous outing is check the websites of the potholing clubs to find out when the next meet is.

Looking at Gaping Gill from the surface doesn't do it any justice at all. There's a hole in the ground, but only the warning signs and fence offer clues as to its true significance. Down that hole is a 100m drop. At the bottom of the drop is a cavern that could easily hold York Minster. Waterfalls plunge down into this magnificent underground space, creating a visual and aural environment that has few rivals.

Huge pothole network
beneath the Yorkshire Dales

Contains the country's
highest waterfall

Winched access to
the cave two weeks
a year during meets
organised by
local clubs

When the winch meets take place, the area is home to a camp of caving volunteers who look after visitors above and below the ground. Ingleborough – one of Yorkshire's famous Three Peaks – looms in the distance and limestone pavements and outcrops dot the landscape. It's this limestone environment, so typical of the Yorkshire Dales, that enabled Gaping Gill to be formed by erosion over thousands of years.

It's quite difficult to reach and you'll need to make sure you're kitted out correctly. For the hiking section make sure you've got good-quality walking boots. For the descent and ascent at Gaping Gill, you could do with waterproofs if you're averse to getting a bit wet.

Clapham is the easiest place to start making your way up to Gaping Gill. There's a decent-sized car park in the village; another option is to head to Clapham railway station, which is a short walk away. Follow the signs for Ingleborough Cave – another underground attraction detailed in this book – which can be visited on the same day if you set off early. From the village, follow the nature trail and continue on the path beyond the cave. You'll eventually have a steep climb up some rocks; continue ahead and turn left at the stile to reach Gaping Gill. There'll probably be a few people making the trek with you, and it will be obvious where to head when you see the tents.

When you register and pay (cash only), you'll be given a wristband with a number on. It's a safety measure to make sure nobody is left down in the pothole, but it also indicates when it will be your time to descend. It takes a few minutes to winch one person down Gaping Gill and bring somebody else back up in the single seat, so only around 20 people will get down there in an hour. At busy times, this can mean a wait of an hour or two. You can check the club's Twitter account to see how busy it is as they will post regular updates during the winch meets.

When your number is displayed, it's time to make your way to the temporary platform that will have been built across the top of Gaping Gill. A few safety instructions are explained as you take the seat – mainly warnings to keep your arms and legs in – and then you get strapped in. The floor of the platform is then slid away and it's perhaps not a good idea to look down at this point because you'll get the first idea of how deep this Yorkshire hole in the ground actually is.

previous pages The opening to Gaping Gill on the surface offers no hint of the wonders below.

As the chair starts to take you down, deep into the ground, your senses will pick up a variety of features. It all happens so quickly, but there are many things to register. You pass different layers of rock. There are various types of vegetation. The waterfall pretty much follows your path down. The cavern below begins to open up. There are multiple waterfalls crashing to the bottom.

When you arrive at the bottom, your safety bar will be unlocked and you can get out of the chair. A member of the potholing club will then take you on a tour of Gaping Gill, pointing out all the different ways experienced cavers can reach this massive chamber. It's quite amazing how busy it is down there when the meet is on; people appear with torchlights from all kinds of nooks and crannies. Others make their own, gruelling way to the surface using only ropes.

The experience at the bottom of Gaping Gill is unforgettable. Looking up towards the hole at the top, you can make out the chair descending through the noisy, splashing waterfalls. After having a good look around, people wishing to go back up join the queue and wait. It's one of the best lines to stand about in – the view is amazing.

below All poised and ready to go, visitors to Gaping Gill are winched down and up one at a time.

GOING DEEPER...

Fell Beck looks like a normal hillside river as it gently flows away from Ingleborough. At Gaping Gill, however, it cascades down the highest unbroken waterfall in the United Kingdom – all out of sight of those walking on the surface. The cave network that leads away from Gaping Gill is extensive, and the first person to reach the floor of the chamber was a pioneering French speleologist. Édouard-Alfred Martel made descents into thousands of caves around the world and was responsible for the study of caves becoming a specific area of scientific research. In 1895 he established the Speleological Society and began writing a newsletter called *Spelunca*. And in that year he made his visit to North Yorkshire, determined to reveal the mysteries of Gaping Gill.

Martel was not the first person to attempt an ascent into Gaping Gill. A local man from Settle, John Birkbeck, had his first shot in 1842. At that time, many locals believed it was a bottomless pit. On two occasions, Birkbeck was lowered into the pothole, but problems with a fraying rope caused the adventure to be abandoned both times. He managed to get 55m down into Gaping Gill, reaching a ledge that is still named after him. When Martel arrived in 1985, he used ropes and ladders to make it all the way to the bottom and was the first person to stand in the huge underground space.

above The incredible descent into Gaping Gill can only be made during two weeks of the year with the help of caving clubs.

We now know that this cave system contains over 16.5km of passages and has a vertical range of over 200m. Until recently, it was possible for serious cavers to tackle the strenuous route from Gaping Gill to Ingleborough Cave, although a rock fall has now sealed off that path. Many of the passages are difficult and very dangerous – especially following heavy rain. The caving system can flood dangerously. Following exceptionally heavy periods of rain, the water can back up into the main chamber and create a lake several metres deep. If this happens during the winch meets, visits down Gaping Gill will be suspended.

LOCATION	OPENING HOURS Daily	ADDRESS 53–55 Lime Street,	EMAIL admin@ouse	THE LOWDOWN
Newcastle,	tours (must be	Ouseburn Valley, Newcastle	burntrust.org.uk	
off the A193	booked in advance).	upon Tyne, NE1 2PQ	WEBSITE www.ouse	
on Lime Street	PRICE £7/£4	TEL 0191 261 6596	burntrust.org.uk	

09
VICTORIA TUNNEL

A FORGOTTEN PROJECT THAT SHELTERED THOUSANDS

Named after the young queen crowned five years earlier, Newcastle's Victoria Tunnel opened in 1842 with a grand celebration. There was a cannon salute and a party for the workers in Bigg Market. Local dignitaries were treated to an underground ride in a decorated wagon complete with a small orchestra. The route of Victoria Tunnel passes beneath the centre of the city and emerges close to the river Tyne. Visitors to the tunnel in the 21st century will realise that they are just a short walk from an incredible view of Newcastle's famous bridges – a location that has proved so significant to the tunnel in its various guises over the decades.

Free parking is available near the tour's meeting point on Lime Street. If you're not lucky enough to get one of those spots, there are road signs to car parks not too far away. Initially the tour group sits down to listen to a brief introductory talk about where the tour goes and with relevant safety information for when you're underground. Make use of the toilets while you're in the Lime Street office because there are none in the tunnel

49

4km tunnel dug through boulder clay to transport coal wagons from a colliery to the river

Closed after just 18 years and then forgotten about for decades

Converted to an air-raid shelter which could house up to 9,000 people during World War II

and you'll be out for just over two hours if you're on the full tour. There is a shorter one-hour tour for families, and if this sounds more appropriate you can select it when you book online. After being given a torch, it's time to head off with your guide on the short walk to the tunnel entrance.

The original tunnel was 4km long, and 700m of it has remained accessible for the public to explore today. It was constructed to transport coal from the Spital Tongues Colliery down to the ships waiting at jetties on the Tyne. It gently slopes at a one-in-ninety gradient, and wagons full of coal attached to a rope would have made their way down the tracks using nothing but gravity. The wagons were then hauled back up to the colliery with the help of a steam-powered winding engine. The tunnel's use as a conduit for raw materials was short lived, however. The coal extracted was not of great quality and the supply from Spital Tongues eventually ran dry. After just 18 years of transporting coal beneath the buildings of Newcastle, the rumbling of the wagons stopped in 1860 and the city quite literally forgot about the Victoria Tunnel.

Inside the tunnel, you're shown the remains of a bell system that used to notify workers at the head of the tunnel when to begin winding the wagons back up. You'll also see a diagram showing the size of the wagons and how they were designed to perfectly fit into the tunnel. With the help of some audio effects, the guide performs an impressive dramatisation of a fatal accident inside the tunnel when a runaway wagon hurtled down the track. There was simply nowhere to escape to at the side of the tunnel as the wagons were almost as wide as this brick-lined oval hollow dug through boulder clay beneath Newcastle.

During air raids, up to 9,000 people could take shelter in this enclosed environment, and the conditions were tough.

By the late 1930s, with the shadow of war hanging over Europe, British cities were instructed to explore what provision they could make for public shelters in the event of an air raid. While folk in Newcastle had heard about a Victorian tunnel linking two parts of the city, nobody really knew what route it took. A working group took a couple of weeks to identify exactly where the tunnel ran and a plan was devised to install 16 entrances so people would be able to quickly escape the German Blitz. In the end, financial restraints and construc-

previous page The Victoria Tunnel started life as a passage for transporting coal but was later used as a life saver in the Blitz.

tion difficulties meant that only seven entrances were built. It's through one of these that you descend to enter this tunnel-turned-lifesaving shelter beneath Newcastle.

The tunnel is cramped in places. Walking through it means regularly scraping your hard hat on the roof if you're six feet or taller. During air raids, up to 9,000 people could take shelter in this enclosed environment, and the conditions were tough. When an inspector of air raids arrived at the Victoria Tunnel, he was not impressed. The Newcastle shelter had a very poor reputation in comparison with large-scale shelters elsewhere in the country. But it was a life-or-death situation, and many residents were only too happy to head down into Victoria Tunnel when the sirens sounded.

GOING DEEPER...

The name William Gilhespie may not be as well known in the engineering world as that of Brunel or Stephenson. But it was this local man who had the vision to tunnel beneath Newcastle and solve the industrial problem of getting coal from Spital Tongues to the river so that it could be shipped away. It would have been far too costly to haul the coal through the streets, and horse-drawn carts were the last thing wealthy

below Tours into the tunnel are given by informed guides who immerse you in history.

home owners wanted to see outside their property. Putting the operation below ground was an ideal solution, especially as the downhill route enabled gravity to do the hard work.

The Spital Tongues mining operation did not bring the long-term economic riches that had been hoped for, but a century after digging ceased, Victoria Tunnel had its finest hour saving thousands of lives from the Luftwaffe. Benches were placed along its length to accommodate those taking shelter, but the ones you see in there today were actually installed for a BBC drama. Look carefully at the floor, though, and you can see the holes in the concrete where the original seats were placed. Also look out for the areas where the brick roof is painted yellow instead of white. This special coat was put on because it would react and change colour to pink in the event of a gas attack by the German planes. Thankfully, this never happened. If it had, the warning given by the paint would likely have come too late for those in the shelter, but it would have alerted any rescuers arriving afterwards in time to save themselves.

The walk through the tunnel takes you past several blast walls, added to prevent explosions spreading along the straight tunnel. The furthest point of the underground tour is the spot where sheltering folk went to spend a penny. This was not a glamorous area, consisting of several rather simple open-topped metal cylinders that served as makeshift toilets. Their imprint can still be seen on the tunnel floor, and an original loo remains to give an idea of what this area must have been like. These toilets were curtained off to give at least some element of privacy, but the prospect of up to 9,000 people coming here to use the facilities would not have been pleasant. Ladies and gents used different areas, separated by a blast wall. You can still see a section of the 'Ladies' sign painted on the wall. Nearby, some steps rise to an entrance at street level, and it's here the full toilets were carried up to by the air-raid shelter warden. In what was definitely not the most inspiring part of the job, he would have had to empty the waste at the surface, add chemicals and return the containers for others to use.

below Although a tragic 19th century accident resulted in loss of life, countless people were saved by the tunnel in the war years.

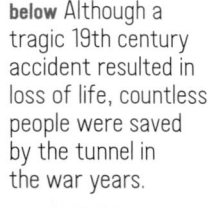

LOCATION	OPENING HOURS Mar –	PRICE £19/£14/£11, family	TEL 0191 370 4000
North of	Oct 10–5; end of Oct	£49.50. Admission gives	EMAIL museum@beamish.
Durham,	to late Mar 10–4;	access for 12 months	org.uk
off the	closed selected days	ADDRESS Beamish, County	WEBSITE www.beamish.
A693	in Jan and Feb	Durham, DH9 0RG	org.uk

THE LOWDOWN

10 BEAMISH DRIFT MINE

STEP BACK IN TIME

Beamish is an immersive historical experience on a grand scale. A favourite with junior school teachers organising days out, the large site is split into different zones, each with a focus on a different era. Original electric trams brought in from Sheffield and other cities connect each attraction on a circular route, with stops for 1820s Pockerley Hall, a Victorian town and a 1940s farm. There's much fun to be had by all ages after changing modern money at the bank for older currency. You can then go and spend it in the old sweet shop, buy some broken biscuits, taste some freshly baked bread and enjoy fish and chips for dinner. But it's the 1900s pit village and colliery that holds the biggest interest for those exploring underground as it's at this tram stop where you'll be able to explore an early-20th-century drift mine.

Groups are taken on a walking tour to the coal face every 15 minutes or so. As it is a drift mine, the entrance is a passageway into the side of the hill that takes you to where the miners used to work to bring out coal. There's no need to go deep underground using a mineshaft to take a look at the working condi-

above There's plenty to do above ground at Beamish too, exploring how we used to live in decades past.

previous page Generations of men made their living bringing coal to the surface.

tions for those who earned a living here. But be warned that getting into the drift mine can be difficult for some because of the very low roof. The further in you go, the more you'll have to crouch. However, if the cramped conditions become too much, you're free to leave at any time and make your own way out of the mine.

Before heading underground, it's a good idea to spend time looking around the pit village. Exploring the buildings that were located close to this working coal mine gives a clearer picture of what life was like here in the 1900s – for that is the era in which this fabulous Beamish experience has been frozen in time. The miners' cottages are cramped but cosy, although a long way from the luxury homes of the better-off dentist and piano teacher over in the town. In the lamp cabin you'll gain an insight into the history of the safety light, where they were stored and how up to 300 of them needed cleaning here every day when the colliery was in use. Don't miss the winding engine house either, as it is the only surviving one of its kind in the Northeast and therefore one of the most prized exhibits in Beamish. But best of all for the youngsters is a visit to the school to see what the children got up to while their fathers were down the pit. This is where the '3Rs' were drilled into the youngsters of the Victorian era, and a stern teacher may still be spotted patrolling the corridors. When you've finished writing on slate boards, head out into the yard for break and see if you can get the hang of a booler – an old toy hoop with a handle attached to roll it along the ground. It's a lot harder than it looks.

The meeting point for the walk into the drift mine is next to the lamp cabin. Tours are given regularly throughout the day – the last one is 30 minutes before closing time. There may be a short wait until the next group departs, but this gives you a chance to chat with the guide and find a hard hat that fits properly. The mine opened in 1855, with 1913 being the peak production year for the colliery. As you head into it, you immediately get a feel for how dark and cramped the conditions were for those working here all their lives. It's not unusual to see some of your group turn around before long and head back to the surface. Things only get more squashed as you head deeper underground. There is plenty to listen to from the guide during the tour along the mine, about how

below You'll need to stoop to enter the drift mine and experience the 19th century working conditions.

harsh life was from a very young age during the 19th century, the high amount of illness that accompanied life in the mine, the low life expectancy and the contrast with modern mining. But despite the harsh working and living conditions, there was a deep sense of community in these parts. Miners who worked down here over a century ago looked out for each other and did their best to keep everybody safe.

GOING DEEPER...

The vision for creating the Beamish Museum and for bringing the industrial heritage of the Northeast to life came from York-shireman Frank Atkinson. A huge fan of museums since he was a young boy, Atkinson was inspired by the open-air folk and heritage centres of Scandinavia. While touring Norway and Sweden in 1952, he was greatly impressed by the success of these popular folk museums, and he admired how they were given the space to keep alive many countryside traditions and ways of life that would otherwise have died out. On returning to the UK, he saw the potential for developing an outdoor visitor attraction that would fulfil a similar aim.

below The underground environment is a good place to reflect on how tough life was for those earning a crust here.

In the late 1950s, Atkinson was concerned that the northeast region was quickly losing its identity as industries such as coal mining and shipbuilding declined. His proposal was to create a museum about everyday life in the region, and he appealed to the public for donations of relevant items. Anything they could

contribute was collected – and the number of items donated was staggering. The early collection filled 22 huts, and by 1971 a small exhibition was opened at Beamish. The first tram set off in 1973, with Rowley Station being opened three years later at a ceremony involving Sir John Betjeman. New buildings have been added at Beamish every few years since, with recent additions being the church, the chemist and the silver band hall. Plans are currently underway to introduce a 1950s town and an upland farm.

After taking the helm in 1970, Frank Atkinson saw his dream for the Beamish project grow and grow. By 1978, the museum had already welcomed its millionth visitor. In 1987, he retired from the attraction he had founded and in that same year it scooped the award for European Museum of the Year. In the 1995 New Year Honours List, Atkinson was given a CBE – it was the year of Beamish's 25th anniversary as well as the year that would see the 1800s brought to life as Pockerley Old Hall opened. Frank Atkinson died in 2014, but he had lived to see his ambition realised of Beamish becoming a museum about local people, housing many objects donated by the ordinary folk of the Northeast.

above It's hard hats on for all visitors as they head into the mine and hear stories about the northeast's once thriving coal industry.

YORK COLD WAR BUNKER

HOW TO MONITOR A NUCLEAR WAR FROM YORKSHIRE

Climbing the steps to go inside this relatively recent English Heritage acquisition is all well and good as a tourist, but nobody would have relished closing the door behind them in the event of an imminent nuclear attack. This was one of 31 bunkers that would have been staffed by 60 Royal Observer Corps (ROC) volunteers if the worst came to the worst. Should the 'four-minute warning' have sounded, these specially selected volunteers would have been expected to instantly leave their families and head underground. Their job would have been to help monitor where the bombs fell and track the deadly fallout that would hit Britain in the weeks after the blasts. Life inside the York bunker would have been grim for those spending the required 30 days in it – it was certainly not designed as a safe haven for those volunteers, unlike well-resourced bunkers designed for government officials. What's more, no provision was made for them after their important work was finished. When the 30 days were up, they would simply have had to leave the bunker and fend for themselves, like everyone else.

The tours around this remarkable remnant of the Cold War run on the hour, and it's well worth timing your arrival to fit one in. There are information points dotted around where you can read about the technology employed here and about what life would have been like for those confined within the walls, but there's nothing like having one of the bunker's English Heritage guides to give you the background story and answer the questions you'll inevitably want to ask.

Cold War bunker in active service from the 1960s to the 1990s

Designed for volunteers to monitor fallout in the aftermath of a nuclear war

The most recently built property owned by English Heritage

The most intriguing thing about the bunker is how poorly thought out it was. It lacked equipment and had potentially massive design faults, with the government at the time seeming to be happy to cut corners with this regional resource. For instance, one volunteer inside the bunker would have had to venture out every 12 hours to change monitoring equipment, potentially thereby being exposed to life-threatening radiation levels. But those in charge didn't waste money on providing radiation suits for those stationed here. Instead, they would have gone out into the post-nuclear wasteland with only a scarf around their mouths. The decontamination shower you see by the main door looks similarly comically inadequate by today's standards its hand-held nozzle having very slim chance of getting all the radioactive material off the person using it. The bunker was built in the 1950s to withstand a two-megaton blast from eight miles away. But as the size of weapons increased in the 1960s it was not even certain the structure would survive an initial attack. Throughout the Cold War, volunteers came in to monitor and check the building on a regular basis – including on Bonfire Night, when fireworks would play havoc with one of the computer monitors. The York bunker tour reveals these disturbing ironies in the gripping context of the political turmoil that existed at the time.

The Cold War bunker workforce would have been split into three units, each unit dividing the day into sections spent in the three different parts of the secret building. Look out for the canteen, where the inhabitants would take it in turns to entertain themselves and share low-calorie rations. In the cramped dormitories, imagine the difficulty of getting to sleep with the hum of the generator in the background and the occasional noisy outburst from the pressurised sewage system. The hub of the bunker was the operations room. Here, readings would be exchanged with other monitoring stations and the location

opposite Chillingly untouched, the York bunker was designed to relay terrifying news of apocalypse across the country.

11 YORK COLD WAR BUNKER

of bomb blasts triangulated. The walls in here were painted brown and blue, apparently to make people feel happy and focused (two attributes that would have been in short supply among any post-nuclear volunteers even with a less drab choice of colour scheme).

As part of the tour, a ten-minute film is shown while you sit on the original government chairs used here during the Cold War. It's not for the squeamish, showing as it does the impact of nuclear blasts on buildings and people. But it does provide context for anybody young enough not to have lived through what was at times a frightening period. At the end of the tour, you emerge into fresh air and share a sense of relief with the rest of the group that this building never had to be fully used.

GOING DEEPER...

The role of those working in the operations room was to plot where nuclear explosions had taken place and monitor the route of the associated fallout. Glass maps were in place, ready to show the cities that had been struck, while special pens would allow the plotters to show the fallout trail. The word nobody in the room wanted to hear was 'Tocsin'. This was the

below It's doubtful whether the mound would have even survived a nuclear blast.

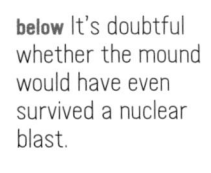

codeword one of the plotters would shout out when they had confirmation of a nuclear attack. As the fallout was plotted, information could be passed to other centres and warnings would be issued to the public when necessary.

As well as the manual monitoring that the Royal Observer Corps (ROC) volunteers would carry out over a period of 30 days, US-built remote sensing devices were installed at 13 of the ROC headquarters. These Atomic Weapons Detection Recognition and Estimation of Yield devices (each simply known as AWDREY) were linked to a sensor on the roof. If an attack had taken place, AWDREY would have automatically kicked in and started to relay information to all the other linked headquarters.

> The word nobody in the room wanted to hear was 'Tocsin'. This was the codeword one of the plotters would shout out when they had confirmation of a nuclear attack.

Thankfully, the ROC was never called upon to get stuck in and man the Cold War bunker. It remains a monument to what might have been and to the madness of any nuclear attack. The Cold War period saw tensions between the East and West warm and chill over the years, with global fears peaking around the time of the Cuban Missile Crisis. Towards the end of the 1980s the Soviet-led Eastern Bloc began to collapse, with one revolution following another, and in 1989 the Berlin Wall fell. The end of the Cold War eliminated the need for the York bunker, and it was decommissioned in 1991.

The bunker was left unused until 2000, when English Heritage took it over. The damp conditions and lack of maintenance had taken their toll on some of the rooms. Paint was peeling, some of the equipment had gone rusty and in some places fungus was found growing on the walls. The extensive restoration work conducted by English Heritage has allowed visitors to get an accurate picture of what was once a top-secret installation designed to minimise the impact of a devastating nuclear war.

Images of how the Yorkshire region would cope if it was thrust into a nuclear conflict shocked viewers in the 1980s when the BBC broadcast *Threads*. Written by Barry Hines, who also penned the much less harrowing *Kes*, *Threads* tells the story of how life falls apart when RAF Finningley is hit by a warhead. One aspect of the film's plot follows an underground emergency operations team trying to coordinate relief efforts and warn people about fallout using short wave radios. The team in the film die in their bunker, having little impact on surface life, which is ravaged by nuclear winter, lawlessness and disease.

12 JORVIK VIKING CENTRE

A VIKING ATTACK ON THE SENSES

Descending the staircase at the Jorvik Viking Centre is like taking a journey back in time. After leaving bustling Coppergate and buying a ticket in the small reception area, you'll make your way down these steps towards the exhibits. Although it's not the country's deepest underground attraction, it's fascinating to see how far down you have to go before reaching what was the street level in Viking days. Over the centuries since the Norse men attacked York in November of AD 866, the surface of the city has risen by six and a half metres. By venturing down the same distance, you will find yourself at the level of the Vikings over 1,000 years ago. This historical gold mine was only fully explored by archaeologists in the 1970s when plans for the nearby shopping centre were being drawn up. A chart on the way down gives an insight into the way in which artefacts from the different ages are found at various levels below the streets of York. Each step taken transports you back in time through the centuries, touching on the Stuart, Elizabethan, Tudor and other eras before being welcomed into Viking Coppergate.

THE LOWDOWN

LOCATION In the middle of Coppergate shopping centre, signed from York centre

OPENING HOURS Apr–Oct 10–5; Nov–Mar 10–4

PRICE £11/£9/£8, family £32/£36. Admission gives access for 12 months

ADDRESS Jorvik Viking Centre, Coppergate Shopping Centre, York, YO1 9WT

TEL 01904 615505

EMAIL Jorvik@ yorkat.co.uk

WEBSITE www. jorvikviking centre. co.uk

The large, jaw-dropping room at Viking street level is a phenomenal window into history, quite literally, for the floor is made from glass, encouraging you to gaze down at the remains of the Viking settlement beneath it. Walk over the glass to see the foundations of different buildings: wooden beams are visible *in situ*, left where the archaeologists found them and allowing 21st-century visitors to see where 9th-century buildings were constructed. Queues often form over the glass as people eagerly wait to head into the main part of the centre, but it's important not to rush. Don't join the queue straight away. Instead, explore this link with the past in detail before moving on. Some folk enjoy this room on their hands and knees to get a close look at the wooden remains, which are unusually well preserved because of the wet conditions they have been kept in beneath York and because they have not been exposed to oxygen over the years.

The next part of the visit is what the Jorvik Viking Centre is famous for – a ride through a reconstructed Viking village as it would have appeared in AD 960. Vehicles holding up to six people slowly transport you past houses and animated Viking models, while an audio guide feeds you information from speakers next to your headrest. There are several languages available for the audio guide, as well as a children's version for younger members of your group. While you should have no problem listening to your chosen version, you may also be able to pick up bits from the recording being played next to you, so, if possible, it may be better to listen to the same version.

Beginning with a darkened journey back through the years, your historical ride turns a corner and enters Jorvik. The story you're told about the life of these Viking invaders is brought to life wonderfully by what you can see around you. There are 31 animatronic Vikings looking convincingly real, most

opposite
York celebrates its heritage at the annual Jorvik Viking festival.

below Historic remains tell us plenty about Viking life.

12 JORVIK VIKING CENTRE

above Your journey through Jorvik introduces intriguing smells and shows the city's original layout.

hauntingly a 46-year-old arthritic woman who has been modelled on a skeleton found on the site. On the journey, try and spot the Viking who is actually a human hidden among the models. Given that the moving models are of a very high standard, this is much trickier than it sounds. The information you're given about these Vikings, their trades and pastimes is all based upon artefacts found where they stand. So, a Viking family making clothes is featured close to where evidence of dyes of different colours was discovered. Children play early board games with their family close to the spot where counters were found. Remains of animals point to an area where people traded fish and meat, while elsewhere shoemaking took place. There is also archaeological evidence of slavery. The one thing you're sure to remember is the smell. As you travel slowly by piles of meat, people working with leather or Vikings on the toilet, the smells change accordingly and play a very important role in this being an immersive historical experience.

After the ride around the village, there's a chance to look more closely at artefacts discovered beneath York in the part of the attraction most akin to a museum. There are many

different items to marvel at, including intricate combs made from antlers, a hoard of coins, weapons, and wooden ice skates that strapped to the bottom of leather shoes. Bringing these items to life, a member of staff in Scandinavian garb is on hand to talk about interesting uses of some artefacts. You are allowed to handle a selection of them. By the time you emerge back at Coppergate's 21st-century street level, you feel as if you have been on a journey both underground and back in time.

above Animated Vikings tell their stories as you pass, but will you be able to spot the one genuine human among them?

GOING DEEPER...

The waterlogged, oxygen-free soil beneath York is the main reason a treasure trove of Viking artefacts survived in such a well-preserved condition. Without oxygen, the wooden items did not rot away, but remained intact. Ironically, though, modern-day influxes of water have led to huge problems at the Viking Centre and caused it to close its doors for over a year. The river Ouse has a history of flooding this great Yorkshire city, and water levels became dangerously high in 2015 during the rainy days following Christmas. Thankfully, warnings were given about possible flooding and emergency action was taken at Jorvik when the water levels started to rise. The precious Viking artefacts were rescued and removed from the danger area, along with well-preserved timbers found on the site and the time capsules that transport visitors around the village. Nevertheless, the flood caused a huge amount of damage, leading to a £4 million re-imagining which saw the visitor experience developed, and the doors opened once more in April 2017. Almost all of the Jorvik Viking Centre was updated, and the aim throughout the restoration was to keep true to the core archaeological storytelling values of the original attraction that opened in 1984. Back then, the queues to see the newly unearthed Viking treasures stretched out of the door and a long way along Coppergate. The site's popularity hit the national news. Today, pre-booking a timeslot on the internet will take you back to AD 960 in a much swifter fashion.

opposite York celebrates its heritage every year at the Jorvik Viking festival.

below Viking treasures hidden for centuries now help us understand their history.

THE MIDLANDS

THE SMALL PEAK DISTRICT VILLAGE of Castleton is a hot spot for magnificent underground spaces. It's found in the southern region of the Peak District National Park known as the 'White Peak' because of the lightly-coloured limestone found there. And it's this porous rock, so susceptible to erosion, that has carved out the deep subterranean wonders found at Treak Cliff Cavern, where the rare Blue John stone is still mined to this day. Nearby in the village, there are stalactites and stalagmites for all to see at The Devil's Arse (more courteously known as Peak Cavern) and Speedwell Cavern, where an ill-informed lead mining venture saw miners get to work via an underground water network. Elsewhere in the White Peak, Poole's Cavern offers some of the fastest forming limestone features on the planet, while the area's lead mining history is explored down a mine in Matlock. At Creswell Crags, naturally formed caves were once home to early man, not to mention woolly mammoths, brown bears and lions! During the last ice age, this was about as far north as it was possible for humans to live and evidence is found in the rare cave paintings adorning the walls. The Midlands has some of the most intriguing underground features in the country, thousands of years in the making.

right Get ready to journey beneath The Midlands, where you'll experience otherworldly landscapes and fascinating formations.

THE LOWDOWN

LOCATION Coalbrookdale, north of Ironbridge; good signage along the way

OPENING HOURS Mid-Mar to early Oct, 11–3

PRICE £3.40/£2.95/£2.50; passport tickets (£26.50/£20.50/£16.50) include admission to other Ironbridge museums; family tickets start at £50; discounts available online **ADDRESS** The Tar Tunnel, High Street, Coalport, Shropshire, TF8 7HT

TEL 01952 433424 **EMAIL** tic@ ironbridge.org.uk **WEBSITE** www. ironbridge.org.uk

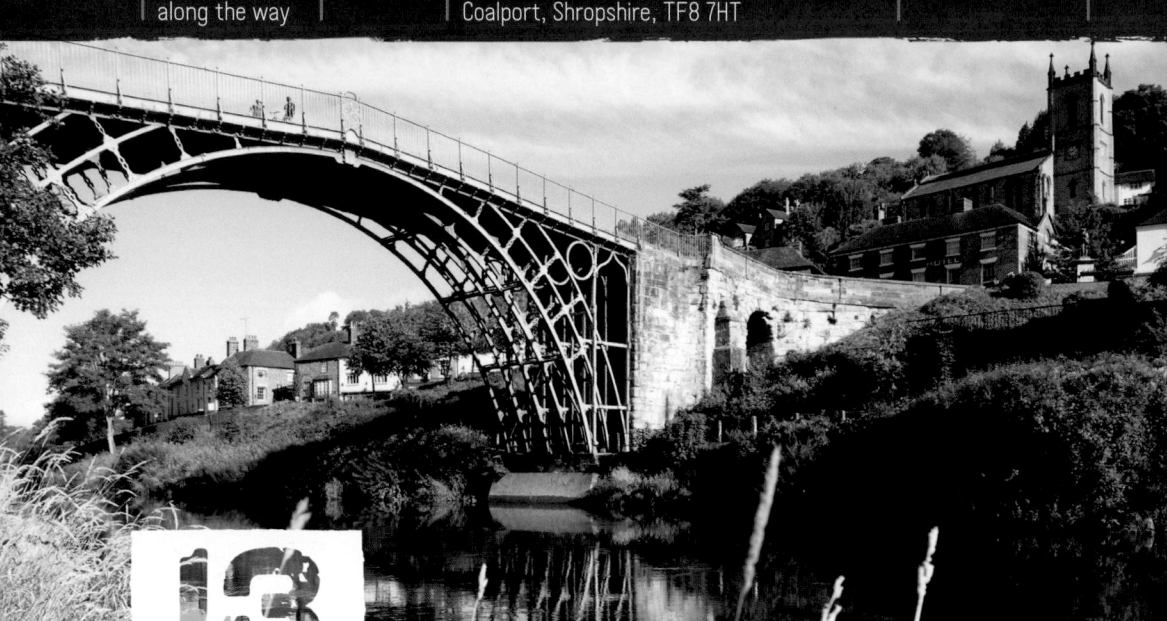

IRONBRIDGE TAR TUNNEL 13

A CHANCE DISCOVERY CHANGES THE PLAN

The Tar Tunnel is one of the ten Ironbridge Gorge attractions which collectively tell the story of how this seemingly quiet valley was at the heart of the Industrial Revolution. Without any doubt at all, the best way to get the most out of your visit is to get the passport ticket which allows entry into all the attractions in and around Ironbridge for twelve months. Together, they build up a picture of what life was like here in the late 18th century and of how the industries were at the cutting edge of new technology. All the museums and attractions feed into each other and work like a historical jigsaw puzzle to show how the different industries were connected and had similarities.

Among the ten museums included on the one Ironbridge passport are the Jackfield Tile Museum, the Coalport China Museum and the Coalbrookdale Museum of Iron. All provide insight into what was made in this part of the world. The best place to start is at the actual iron bridge that gave this place its name. The world's first bridge made from iron, it was a pioneering piece of engineering that made a crucial leap forward in terms of means of crossing the river Severn.

Just down the road from the bridge is the Museum of the Gorge, bringing all the history together and providing a concise overview of why Ironbridge has been designated a UNESCO World Heritage Site.

One of the first things you'll spot inside the Museum of the Gorge is a lengthy and very detailed model of the valley as it would have looked in 1796. At the far side of it, look out for the factories of Coalport at the bottom of the valley and the canal at the top of the hill. Getting coal to these industrial centres from nearby mines was proving a logistically difficult and expensive exercise, so an ambitious solution was sought by William Reynolds, the owner of local ironworks and mines. Reynolds, the man responsible for creating Coalport New Town, proposed to build an underground canal that would directly link industry with the deeper parts of the mine.

You can access the tunnel he built – the Tar Tunnel – by using the free car park just down the road from the Shakespeare Inn at Coalport. There are road signs throughout the World Heritage Site for the Tar Tunnel at Blists Hill. A better

Part of the Ironbridge World Heritage Site celebrating the early days of the Industrial Revolution

The Tar Tunnel was originally dug out to create an underground canal

The accidental discovery of a natural bitumen spring in the 18th century changed its purpose

opposite The famous iron bridge at the centre of the UNESCO World Heritage Site.

below Originally dug to provide transport, the purpose of the tunnel soon changed after the discovery of bitumen.

way to approach this underground engineering marvel is to enjoy a walk along the canal. For a short stroll, park up at the nearby Coalport China Museum and head along the canal side. If you fancy a four-mile loop, begin your walk in the centre of Ironbridge and make your way to the Tar Tunnel by following signs along the river Severn.

These days, the entrance to the Tar Tunnel is about as far from an industrial scene as you can get. A couple of pleasant-looking buildings stand between the canal side and the road. You walk down some steps and go round the back, following the signs to the entrance. After having your ticket stamped, you can head down some steps into a cellar area where, through an archway, you can see the brick-lined tunnel that snakes away before you into the darkness of the hillside and out of sight, and whose extent remained a secret for decades in the early 20th century. Rails along the floor and rusty wagons hark back to the days when this passage was used to move coal. But plans to turn it into a canal were abandoned because of the black stuff oozing from the walls, dripping down over the bricks. The bitumen that gave this tunnel its name still leaves its mark across the 230-year-old brickwork.

GOING DEEPER...

The Tar Tunnel at Ironbridge was born out of a desire to improve transportation. In an age before the railways, great importance was placed on getting coal to factories in a fast and affordable way. The proposed solution at Coalport was to create an underground canal that connected the mines of Blists Hill to the canal running next to the river Severn. Transporting large amounts of coal swiftly and directly from the mine via boat would have been a major boost to the local works when tunnelling began in 1786.

After digging out nearly 300m into the hillside, however, miners came across something they were not expecting – a natural spring of bitumen. This black, sticky material provided industrialist William Reynolds with a business opportunity as it was popular material for weatherproofing ropes and wooden ships. The idea of the underground canal was quickly abandoned and work began on extracting and selling the bitumen. A natural product, bitumen is similar to oil and coal in that it is formed from the remains of plants and animals that lived millions of years ago.

> After digging out nearly 300m into the hillside, miners came across something they were not expecting – a natural spring of bitumen.

above What started out as a coal transportation project soon became a business barrelling bitumen.

And there were great quantities of it within this hillside. When Reynolds began the extraction, 1,000 gallons a week were flowing. The bitumen was placed into barrels and sold off. Some went to local industries and some to companies in London. The operation was short-lived, though. After five years, the rate of bitumen flowing from the spring had significantly slowed and demand for the product started to wane over time.

While developing the bitumen business, William Reynolds came up with another solution to bring coal in quickly and cheaply. He created the Hay Inclined Plane, which can still be seen on the slope outside the tunnel. Linking canals at the top and bottom of the hill, tub boats were hauled out of the water to travel along the incline before being eased into the canal at the other end. Empty boats would travel up to the Shropshire Canal, where they would be filled with coal and transported back down. Reynolds became known for his work on developing canals, with inclines becoming a speciality.

Eventually, tar extraction in the tunnel ceased but the underground passageway continued to be used as a wagon link to the Blists Hill mines. When it finally fell out of use and was sealed off, stories of the Tar Tunnel survived in the local area, and it was remembered as a wondrous invention epitomising the Industrial Revolution. Modern-day confirmation of the Tar Tunnel's location did not come until 1965, when the Shropshire Mining Club explored beyond a door in the cellar of the village shop. Behind mounds of rock at the entrance, they discovered the brick-lined tunnel – and the bitumen still oozing slowly from the walls.

POOLE'S CAVERN

A HUB FOR AMBITIOUS STALAGMITES

Tourists have been taking a peek inside Poole's Cavern for hundreds of years. Its name derives from a legend that it was once the hideout of a local villain named Poole, who is said to have been a 15th-century robber who used the cavern as the base for his ill-doing. In the 17th century, it was included in a famous poem, 'The Wonders of the Peak', by Charles Cotton, and ever since then it has been a popular attraction. When wealthy tourists were taking part in a tour of the Peak District, they would call in at the cavern along with other familiar stops such as Chatsworth, Mam Tor and Peak Cavern.

Back then, anybody wanting to see the stalactites hanging from the roof of the cavern had to crawl through a fairly small hole in order to reach the chamber. Once inside, a local villager would show them the natural wonders by candlelight. There are some reports of profiteering tour guides blowing out their candles when inside and only lighting them again when they had been handed more money. Thankfully, that practice has stopped so there's no need to worry about being plunged into darkness once you're inside. It's possible that Mary Queen of

THE LOWDOWN

LOCATION South-west of Buxton centre, well signed from there and A53

OPENING HOURS Mar-Oct 9.30-5; Nov-Feb 10-4

PRICE £9.95/£8.75/ £5.50, family £27

ADDRESS Poole's Cavern, Green Lane, Buxton, Derbyshire, SK17 9DH

TEL 01298 26978

EMAIL info@poolescavern.co.uk

WEBSITE www. poolescavern.co.uk

Scots was the first famous visitor to arrive at the cavern, but that is up for debate. She was in the area during 1582, though some doubt whether she would have attempted the cramped crawl into the chamber.

These days, a visit to Poole's Cavern doesn't involve any crawling through holes. When the Duke of Devonshire, who owned the land, realised the cavern's potential in 1853, he arranged for the entrance to be blasted open and a path was laid to give comfortable access. There is no need for a hard hat on this cavern tour either. There are only a couple of places where the tallest folk will have to watch their head.

Near the shop there is an exhibition about local geology and how the feature was formed that is worth spending time on when you first arrive. Your guide will then lead you on a small path outside to the entrance of the cavern. The further into the cavern you go, the more magical the features become. The initial stalactites and stalagmites look very impressive, but they are easily outshone by those deeper in. The flowstone in the cavern, formed by calcite within the rainwater that takes twelve hours to filter down from the hill, has also created some amazing shapes. Some of them were so big that they blocked the way through to the deeper parts of the cavern, forming a huge flowstone barrier that the Victorians quickly blew their way through with the help of dynamite.

Look out for the massive seven-foot-long stalactite hanging down above the river, which still flows in winter months. It's known as the Flitch of Bacon, and is so thick it resembles a tree trunk. Sadly, the tip of it was knocked off by visitors to the cavern hundreds of years ago who believed they were retrieving a precious gem. When they realised the calcite tip wasn't valuable at all, they dumped it in a local field. It remained missing until the turn of the 21st century, when somebody digging in their garden discovered it and brought it down to the cavern. The tip can now be seen resting beneath

Limestone cavern featuring sparkling crystal formations

Stalagmites and stalactites form here at a much faster rate than at most other places

Country park, woodland and panoramic peak on the same site

opposite There are incredible formations to be seen all along the cavern's underground passage.

below Fascinating shapes have developed deep below the Peak District.

the stalactite it originally belonged to. It can't be reattached, though, because the huge stalactite has since started to form a new tip.

You'll be asked not to touch the stalagmites, and for good reason. The waterproof nature of human skin can leave the faintest of traces on the rock, and just a few hundred gentle touches can stop the stalagmites from absorbing rainwater. This means they will receive no calcite and grow no more. Later on the tour there are a few 'dead' stalagmites this has happened to that you can touch.

Over 300m of the cavern is open to the public. But the extent of this fascinating network does not stop there. At the end of your tour, you are shown a rock fall which prevented the farthest parts of the cavern being explored. In the late 1990s, a black-and-white video camera was lowered down a hole to film what was behind the rocks – and a new cavern branded 'Seventh Heaven' was discovered. It is thought to be much larger than the one that is open to the public today. Cavers enter Poole's Cavern on most weekends in an attempt to head over the rocks and make their way down into the new, undiscovered part of this underground system.

opposite The default reaction once you're in the Cavern is to gaze up, point and gasp.

below No hard hats are needed here, on a carefully created level route.

GOING DEEPER...

The subterranean wonder beneath Buxton may strike you as a magnificent natural phenomenon, but some of Poole's Cavern's most star-tling features have their roots in human actions. The hill above the cavern is called Grinlow, which you can walk up to enjoy the view. During the 18th century, large quan-tities of lime were burned on Grinlow and used locally in agriculture. Waste lime powder was dumped on land high above the cavern, proving to be a very rich

source of calcite. When rainwater mixed with the powder and then percolated through the ground, it had a very high concentration of calcium carbonate as a result. This is a dream combination when it comes to the formation of stalactites and stalagmites, and the marvels of Poole's Cavern are all down to those 18th-century workers beavering away at the lime kiln, blissfully unaware of the subterranean wonders they were helping to create as they dumped their powdery waste onto Grinlow. But thankfully we get to benefit from seeing the extraordinary calcite formations their waste product helped to create.

There is one particular section within the cavern that has an incredible number of stalagmites. It's above this part of the chamber where the lime powder was tipped. The stalagmites forming here grow at a much faster rate than in other show caves around the country where there is not such a rich source of calcium carbonate. And the results are visible all around you. There are stalagmites growing from practically every nook and cranny you can see in the chamber. When you look down to the ground, there are newly formed stalagmites on what looks like a relatively recently paved pathway. There are even stalagmites beginning their long, upward journey from the metal railings at the side of the path.

below Humans dumping limestone waste above the cavern accelerated stalagmite formation.

Stalagmite growth that would take thousands of years in other parts of the world takes place in a few decades at Poole's Cavern. Research has discovered that these stalagmites in Poole's Cavern can increase in size by as much as 1cm a year. That may not seem a lot when you look at it on a ruler, but the same amount of growth in a different cavern could take several hundred years. This level of accelerated growth makes Poole's Cavern a fascinating place for scientists and well worth the environmental protection it is afforded.

LOCATION Castleton is located on the A6187 between Hathersage and Chapel-en-le-Frith; the cavern is signed from the village

OPENING HOURS Mar–Oct daily, 10–4.20; Nov–Feb daily, 10–3.20

PRICE £9.95/£8.95/ £5.30, family £27.50 **ADDRESS** Treak Cliff Cavern, Buxton Road, Castleton, S33 8WP

TEL 01433 620571 **EMAIL** treakcliff@ bluejohnstone.co.uk **WEBSITE** www. bluejohnstone.co.uk

THE LOWDOWN

IN SEARCH OF A PRECIOUS STONE

The quaint and picturesque village of Castleton is the jewel in the crown of the Peak District National Park. And when it comes to precious stones, this popular tourist honeypot has more than its fair share. Go into any of Castleton's gift shops and you'll find a cache of jewellery on sale. Necklaces, earrings, bracelets and rings – all featuring a dark blue stone with pretty patterns. This is Blue John, and the only place in the world you'll find it is deep inside the hill to the west of the village.

Treak Cliff Cavern is the one location where the rare veins of Blue John are still mined. Standing outside the shops in Castleton's main street, you can see the entrance halfway up the hillside.

Getting to the cavern from the village involves either a short drive following the brown tourist signs or a decent walk from the centre of the village. If you opt for the car, there's plenty of free parking on the road by the entrance. You'll then have a short walk up the hill to the ticket office. Tours head into the cavern regularly, but be prepared for a short wait. Teas and coffees are available – as are toilets – and a bell will ring when it's tour time.

15 TREAK CLIFF CAVERN

Your trip into the depths of Treak Cliff Cavern calls at six different chambers, each of them very different. The first three feature Blue John and are an opportunity to see the rare stone *in situ*. Some of the veins have only recently been discovered. Examples of the blue stone can be seen above your head and to your side on the wall. One huge pillar full of Blue John is said to contain a quantity worth £1 million and weighing the same as four elephants. Other veins are hidden down almost inaccessible passages that, thankfully, you are not required to crawl along.

The second stop on the tour brings you to a cavern rammed full of fossils. Everywhere you look in the limestone walls and roof, fossilised sea creatures abound and remind us of when this part of Derbyshire was on the Equator and under the sea. It's a mesmerising, inspiring space.

The last three caverns you get to see at Treak Cliff are all natural; where the mining heritage ceases, the wonders formed by water take over. Large passages formed by underground rivers allow visitors to gaze up at the circular erosion once caused by subterranean pools. The huge spaces carved out of the rock are quite something. The stars of the tour, however, are the features created by water returning to the cavern, this time carrying minerals leading to the formation of stalactites, stalagmites and glorious flowstone.

The first stalactites you see are relatively small. Those in the final cavern, however, are huge and have taken tens of thousands of years to reach their current length. Stalagmites stretch up from the floor, with one encroaching on a stalactite, the two calcite formations looking like they could almost touch and form a pillar. In reality, that process will take another thousand years. At one point there are nine dumpy stalagmites, curiously nicknamed 'The Seven Dwarves', close to the path, and the tour guide will be happy for you to pat one of these on your way past for good luck. Rain takes a couple of weeks to drip through the limestone and fall in the cavern. There's a high chance of you getting splashed, given the wet local weather. In one section, the dripping of the rainwater and the depositing of its minerals has led to an astonishing flowstone creation resembling the Peak District's own Niagara Falls. Over several different ledges, the flowstone gives the impression that it's cascading down the cavern when it is, of course, solid and unmoving. The mining equipment on display is a reminder of the reason this hillside was explored in the 18th century, but the beauty of the formations within the cavern itself is on a par with that of the Blue John stone those early miners were seeking.

The only place where the rare Blue John stone is currently mined

Guided tour revealing fossils, Blue John stone, stalactites and stalagmites

Occupies a picturesque setting in the heart of the Peak District National Park

GOING DEEPER...

The origins of the name Blue John are not certain. Despite being discovered by a miner who had John as a first name, it's thought that the semi-precious material wasn't named after him. Instead, most explanations look across the English Channel. During the 18th-century reign of Louis XVI of France, some of the Castleton stone was exported to that country. Because there are pretty blue and yellow patterns found on it, the French referred to it using their own words for these colours: *bleu-jaune*. The story goes that when this translation reached the Derbyshire miners, their pronunciation of French words wasn't that good and so it became a very English 'Blue John' stone.

below You'll be able to spot the precious Blue John stone amongst the dazzling fossils and stalactites.

Furnishings and decorations featuring Blue John became fashionable in England during the 18th century and into the 19th. Some of the finest houses in the nation have boasted some Blue John on their tables – including Buckingham Palace and nearby Chatsworth House. All the material used in the creation of these fine decorations, which range from candle holders to ornate bowls, was found in the one hill behind Castleton, known as Treak Cliff Hill. The veins of the Blue John hidden within it are tricky to find because the hill is not exactly brimming with it. Miners in the 18th century who first came across Blue John were not even looking for a new, rare mineral. Instead, they were on the hunt for lead, which was used in many industries at the time and had been found elsewhere in the area. Blue John, however, soon became their new focus.

Historically, only fourteen distinct veins have been identified. They were each given names, such as Millers Vein, Treak Cliff Blue Vein, 5 Vein and 12 Vein. The last major vein of Blue John was discovered in the middle of the 19th century – but all that changed in 2014. Treak Cliff Cavern mine manager Gary Ridley was trying out a new method of mining with a stone chainsaw and saw evidence of crystallisation near a handrail – right on the route taken by visitors. Within a few minutes of using the saw in this location he had uncovered a brand new vein of Blue John. It was the first substantially different deposit of Blue John that had been found in over 150 years, and it had experts very excited. Because the discovery was made close to the tourist route, this new find is one of the features you can see quite clearly when you look around.

right The Hope Valley, formed by huge glaciers and home to several underground adventures.

				THE LOWDOWN
LOCATION On the A6187 to the west of Castleton	**OPENING HOURS** Apr–Oct 10–5; Nov–Mar 10–4; last tour is one hour before closing **PRICE** £12/£11/£10 family £40	**ADDRESS** Winnats Pass, Castleton, Hope Valley, Derbyshire, S33 8WA **TEL** 01433 621888	**EMAIL** info@speed well cavern.co.uk **WEBSITE** www. speedwellcavern. co.uk	

16 SPEEDWELL CAVERN

A SUBTERRANEAN BOAT TRIP

Standing at the entrance to Winnats Pass, just outside Castleton, it's hard not to gawp at the high limestone edges that time has ripped apart, allowing the modest A6187 that goes through the pass to become one of the country's most scenic drives. The steep climb, strewn with fallen limestone rocks at the road-side, inadvertently became one of the principal trans-Pennine routes in 1979 when landslides transformed the main road heading west from Castleton into something resembling an earthquake zone and forced the authorities to close it for good.

Motorists accessing Castleton from the Manchester side of the Peak District now use Winnats Pass, which can be hair-raising at the best of times and downright treacherous in wintery conditions. At the foot of the pass, a whitewashed building announces the location of Speedwell Cavern. In a High Peak village renowned for its caverns – the home of Blue John is not far away – Speedwell stands out as offering something very different. To reach this cavern beneath the rolling Derby-shire hills, you have to take an underground boat ride through a cramped tunnel carved out for 18th-century lead miners. The

Lead mine opened in the 18th century

Underground canal blasted out of the rock, allowing access to lead by boat

Highlight is the huge cavern and 'bottomless pit' at the end of the boat ride

incredible scenery around Winnats Pass may tempt you to don hiking boots and head out onto the hilltops, but the lure of that underground boat ride will most likely prove more powerful. Hiking can wait until you resurface.

If you're lucky there'll be no queues, but on busier days you'll have to wait until a few boat trips have returned to the surface before it's your turn. Family members waiting in line can take it in turns to go and have a look around the small shop, which also sells food and drink. Black-and-white pictures on information boards show TV and film stars of yesteryear who have taken the boat ride – you'll see Paul Newman posing in the car park after a trip to Speedwell and the cast of *Coronation Street* filming here in the 1960s. Whether the cavern is popular with modern-day movie stars is unclear.

Before you go down, you'll be given a hard hat. The protective headgear is not for show or to add to the atmosphere; it's simply that anybody over six feet tall is likely to crack their head on the low ceiling. Waiting for you at the bottom is an underground sight like no other: a small boat sitting on a channel of water, waiting to take you into a tunnel of darkness.

There's a dark humour among many of the guides here at Speedwell, who recount the cavern's history alongside 'jokes' about guides getting lost, groups of students not making it back to the surface and disastrous flooding events. It's not a place for the claustrophobic. The boat fits the width of the channel perfectly, meaning the rocky walls brush the coats of

previous page All aboard for a Peak District boat journey like no other.

right A tight space where boat tours squeeze past each other amongst the limestone tunnels.

those sitting at the edge of the boat. The tallest passengers will feel their hard hats scrape the rock above them. While most children are fine on the voyage, which they rightly see as an adventure, I know grown men who have begged to be taken back at this stage, even asking to swap over onto the boat of an earlier returning party at a passing place. But there is no way out at this stage. And those grown men had to match the bravery of their young children as the boat progressed relentlessly along the dark, tiny channel.

At the end of the waterway, the boat stops and you're faced with the enormity and sheer splendour of the cavern. It is awesome. Cathedral-like. Created by water channels eroding the limestone, it extends far above, and you can make out the plunge pools of the waterfalls that once formed here. Below, it dives down to a small body of water once thought to be bottomless, but in reality just a few metres deep.

It's a surreal underground landscape and one that can't really be imagined by looking at photographs, and certainly not by merely passing the unassuming building at the bottom of Winnats Pass. There are indeed few other places on earth where you can descend into the bedrock to experience an underground boat trip.

above Speedwell Cavern is one of the most popular attractions in the Peak District and lists Paul Newman and the *Coronation Street* cast among celebrity visitors.

GOING DEEPER...

As far as business ideas go, setting up a lead mine at this spot in Castleton was not the greatest enterprise ever undertaken. Operations began to get lead out of the mine at Speedwell in 1771 and continued, at varying rates, for about 20 years. But even though an investment of £14,000 was ploughed into the business in the hope that the lead recovered from under the ground was going to make a fortune, the enterprise turned out to be a folly. In fact, only £3,000 of lead was ever taken from the mine, making it a financial disaster. The first vein of lead tackled by miners only earned £100, with workers operating in difficult conditions during what must have been a challenging period for the owner.

It was the discovery of the Longcliff Vein that led to the recovery of most lead, and the majority of the £3,000 gained was down to this half-mile stretch of lead that is now sealed off because the workings had deteriorated into a dangerous condition. Back in the 18th century, while the lead mining was still under way, interest in this pioneering and unique operation was such that early tourism blossomed, with a steady stream of visitors being taken down and given a tour in a boat while mining was going on around them.

The highlight of the tour then, as it is now, was the area known as the Bottomless Pit, referring to the depths of the cavern in a pool of water some 50m below the viewing area, which itself is 200m beneath the hillside. Miners used this so-called bottomless pit to dump all the material they blasted and dug out when making the Far Canal, which runs boats further into a network of caverns. In total, 2,500 tonnes of rock were cast into the pit, which is covered by a subterranean lake covering some 250 square metres. Experts at the time considered this pit to be 150m deep. In truth, it was maybe around 60m deep at the time, but it has been filled up with so much material that the distance from the surface of the water to the depths of the 'Bottomless Pit' is now only 11m.

The water from the lake in the cavern emerges lower down the hill and closer to the village at Peak Cavern Gorge – and the lake has never run dry in the 450 years it has been monitored.

above Down a long set of stairs, a boatman awaits to take you deep beneath the hill towards the Cavern.

opposite It turns out the "bottomless pit" does have a bottom, but it's a long way down.

17

PEAK CAVERN

INTO THE DEVIL

The car park for Peak Cavern – also known as The Devil's Arse – is found on the main road from Castleton as it heads deeper into the Peak District National Park. From here, there is a decent walk past cosy cottages and alongside a stream up to the entrance to the cavern. Even before you pay to go in, the view of its magnificent entrance is awe-inspiring. The Peak Cavern gapes like a huge, natural mouth about to swallow its visitors, and you cannot help but be drawn inside.

Just inside the entrance, the first part of the tour focuses on the rope-making industry that once thrived here. Families used to live in small rooms right here inside the cave and spent their days twisting long, strong rope that could be used by the lead miners of Derbyshire. Rope ladders and rope to hoist materials up mine shafts were specialities produced here. One of the first things you'll do inside the Peak Cavern is see a rope being made in a traditional way. It's twisted this way and that. Then, with the help of some basic tools and some expert knot-tying, a length of tough, high-quality rope is the finished product. Children started work on this exact spot aged as young as

THE LOWDOWN

LOCATION West of Hope, in the Peak District on the A6187

OPENING HOURS Apr–Oct, hourly tours daily, 10–5; Nov–Mar hourly tours every Sat and Sun 10–5, and Mon–Fri tours at 11 and 2

PRICE £11.25/£10.25/ £9.25 family £37

ADDRESS Peak Cavern Walk, Castleton, Hope Valley, S33 8WS

TEL 01433 620285

EMAIL info@peak cavern.co.uk

WEBSITE www. peakcavern.co.uk

four and were only expected to live until their mid-30s. Life here among the rope-makers was tough. Animal fat was burnt in candles and used to waterproof the rope, making the cavern conditions smoky and reducing visibility significantly. Drinking the water in the stream was dangerous for the workers at the time because it picked up lead content from the hills. It was safer to consume the local ale than it was to quench your thirst with the water, which is why there were once 29 pubs open for business in the tiny village of Castleton.

As you head beyond a gate, you leave the rope-making heritage behind as the tour enters the natural splendour of the cave system. The vast open spaces you see on the second half of the tour are wonderful. Whirling gaps in the limestone above your head were carved out by water thousands of years ago. They're inspiring to gaze at, but don't expect many of the 'pretty' formations you may have seen at other show caves. Some stalactites making unusual shapes can be spotted: the guide will shine a light on Father Christmas and his pet dog, along with a family of rabbits. But many of the finest features disappeared in the Victorian years when profiteering guides cut them down and sold them to visitors. One particularly large piece even made its way to Chatsworth House. Their removal is a tragedy really, when you consider how many thousands of years such features take to form.

Heavy rain sometimes sees the cavern flood. If you're visiting at one of these times, you may find your guide changes the 'cavern tour' to a 'flood tour' and presents you with a really rare sight. Crystal clear water from an underground river encroaches onto what is normally a dry path. Heed the warnings from the guide to tread carefully because it's almost impossible to distin-

opposite Young and old are mesmerised by the scale of Peak Cavern.

below The approach to the country's biggest cave entrance.

17 PEAK CAVERN

guish where the path ends and the water begins, the floodwater is that clear. There are always some people who go home with wet feet. It's at this point you'll discover why this underground attraction has been given its somewhat vulgar nickname.

Queen Victoria visited Peak Cavern twice, the first time in her younger years, and she was not amused when she heard that the attraction went by the name The Devil's Arse. As a result, the name was altered and the less vulgar 'Peak Cavern' was adopted as its name until a rebranding exercise reintroduced the 'Devil's Arse' nickname in 2007. On that first visit, Victoria managed to get in a tiny boat to access the deeper parts of the cave. This was not possible on her second trip to Peak Cavern, when she was carrying more weight. As a result, a passageway was blasted close to where the boat used to travel, allowing easier access on foot. You'll probably have to stoop as you wander through this tiny tunnel, and mind you don't hit your head on the rock. But when Queen Victoria – at 4 feet 9 inches tall – strode through here, she managed to keep her head safe without so much as bending her knee.

below At Christmas time, the Peak Cavern is transformed into a jolly concert venue, with hundreds of carollers and a brass band creating angelic tunes.

A fence blocks the way when you reach the farthest extent of the tour. Beyond it, you can see a strange wooden slide disappearing down into the darkness. On first sight, you may think it was apparatus for centuries-old mine-workings, but it was actually for transporting the former *Doctor Who* actor, Tom

Baker. It was built for the BBC TV series *The Silver Chair*, part of the *Chronicles of Narnia*. Baker's character whizzed down it into the cave. Even though you won't come out in a fictional country, it is still possible to go beyond the fence and explore some of the cave network that lies beyond the standard tour. A bespoke underground caving adventure can be booked with Peak Instruction. On this tour, experts will provide all the equipment you need and take you to places few have seen. For more information, visit www.peakinstruction. com or find @caverpete on Twitter.

above You'll probably have to crouch to reach the end of the tour – a hardship not suffered by the diminutive Queen Victoria.

GOING DEEPER...

Christmas is a great time to visit the Peak Cavern. It may be colder, and you will almost certainly need your thermals, but it's a month when you can join in with what has become a fantastic Castleton tradition: Carols in the Cavern. Creating a perfect festive atmosphere, the concert seats hundreds of carollers in front of a brass band. All are protected from the elements by the roof of the cavern, although there may be a few drops of water dripping out of the limestone and landing on your head as you sing 'Silent Night'. Derbyshire brass bands take it in turns over several nights to play Christmas favourites for the singing visitors, who have been warmed up on arrival with a mince pie and some mulled wine. Acoustically, the cavern makes a wonderful concert venue. When decked with fairy lights and Christmas trees, it's a highly welcoming and memorable environment. But if sitting about in the cold isn't your thing, maybe you should check out the concerts held in the summer. Singers who have belted out tunes in this underground venue include Richard Hawley and Lucy Spraggan.

Peak Cavern has featured in the *Most Haunted* TV series, and believers in the paranormal should ask their guide about the local ghost stories. Some guides will speak sincerely about regular encounters with Victorian spirits and will recount how a pair of ghosts have often been sighted running away from tour groups, giving this subterranean adventure the air of a Derbyshire-based X-File.

18 PEAK DISTRICT LEAD MINING MUSEUM

IN THE FOOTSTEPS OF LEAD MINERS

The Peak District Lead Mining Museum is based in the fabulous pavilion building that occupies pride of place next to the river in Matlock Bath. This is a settlement that developed as a Victorian spa town and that over time became known as an inland 'seaside resort' – a reputation that it still enjoys today. The line of shops sitting on just one side of the main street give the town a coastal feel, enhanced by the generous number of them that sell ice cream and fish and chips. There are other popular attractions in Matlock Bath that pull in the visitors, but the town's historical and geological importance is best appreciated at the Lead Mining Museum.

There are two levels of entry. You can pay just to go around the museum, studying the historical mining artefacts and nuggets of information about the Peak District mines. Or, for a little extra, you can upgrade to include one of the tours that investigate Temple Mine. If you're able to manage a short, steep walk up a hill and spend a bit of time crouching in a cramped tunnel, the mine tour offers good value for money and is an excellent way to spend an hour. But make sure you contact the museum in advance to book a place on one of the tours, because they can fill up and numbers are restricted for health and safety reasons. It's well worth combining the museum visit with the underground tour as it brings the 1920s mining operations to life in an impressive way.

Provides insight into the tough life of a Derbyshire lead miner

The Howie Mineral Collection in the museum features specimens from around the world

Guided tours to a 1920s lead mine allow visitors to experience working conditions

The museum takes around an hour to enjoy, and it's best to factor in time to look round the exhibits before you go on the underground tour. That way, before you enter the mine you can get a feel for the history of mining in and around Matlock, for the mining methods that were used and for how the lead was extracted from the local stone. With plenty of written information and a wealth of exhibits dating back to the 18th century, you probably won't get to see everything in detail. But do find time to look at how lighting has changed in mining, with one display comparing modern battery lights with the candle holders used over 200 years ago. And don't forget to make time for the incredible collection of rocks and minerals. There are some on display that are truly mesmerising, including a petrified piece of an oak tree and impressive calcite formations. Children gravitate towards the mocked-up lead mine shafts, which are a squeeze for adults but still worth a go. And don't miss the stained-glass window depicting life in Matlock – complete with fish and chips, ice cream and bikers!

When it's time to gather for the mine tour, you'll be led out of the building, across the road and up a steep slope to the mine entrance. It's inhabited by cave spiders and bats. You're unlikely to see a bat, but do keep your eyes peeled for the distinctive cave spiders dwelling on cobwebs on the rock walls. On the mine's roof you may even see the orb-weaving spider's egg sacs. These are usually found

opposite Tools from yesteryear still occupy the mine, which is also home to fascinating crystal formations.

below There is original mining equipment in both the mine and the museum.

18 PEAK DISTRICT LEAD MINING MUSEUM

93

at the cave entrance, where the flow of air is greater, and they are an impressive sight.

The first thing you'll discover is how difficult the conditions were that miners worked in during the 1920s; then you'll head up to a mine tunnel dug in the 1950s. The differences between those decades are stark. The tunnel worked by miners in the 1950s has much more head room, and the lighting was also considerably better. Many of the old supports are still in place, and it's so well maintained that it looks as if you're on a film set for an Indiana Jones movie. It's not just about mining on this tour, though. There are some amazing crystal formations, as well as the remains of underground water channels and some wonderful clay on the wall that has been tinged with different colours by the minerals.

And to top it all off, when you emerge into daylight again you can become a real prospector and pan for minerals. This option is available to everyone, and even grumbling adults who reckon it's 'just for the kids' tend to get addicted once they give in and try their hand at panning for lead.

GOING DEEPER...

The Peak District has a rich history of lead mining, dating from the Roman era right up to the closing of the last working mine in the 1950s. The reason the region has plenty of lead is down to its geology. Magma is rich in minerals, and when it seeped into the limestone fissures it resulted in the formation of plentiful supplies of lead. Back then, mining would have started from the surface and followed the direction taken by the veins of lead – which sometimes extended for long distances across the countryside.

below Hoping to strike it rich, junior prospectors pan for Peak District lead.

The most prosperous period of lead mining in these parts was in the 18th century, when the largest amount of ore was recovered and some deeper mines were opened up. A major new development was seen to the north of Matlock Bath at Eyam. But the deeper the mines went, the greater the problem of flooding became. Solutions were sought to tackle the water plaguing miners in the depths of the mines, with drainage tunnels being popular as well as, later, steam-powered pumps.

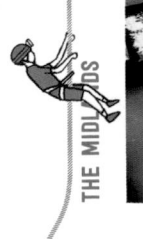

The prospects for lead miners in Derbyshire started to decline in the middle of the 19th century. As well as the price of lead declining, the owners of many mines were seeing the deposits of lead ore becoming exhausted, with the result that few mines were operational by the 20th century. Temple Mine at Matlock Bath was operational for small periods during the 1920s before closing and being reopened for a short run in the 1950s. By then, one mine in Darley Dale was responsible for half the lead ore being mined in this area.

Recently, there has been renewed interest in the Peak District's lead ore deposits, along with fluorspar and calcite. These mineral deposits are needed in a wide range of consumer products and the demand for them is on the increase. Some mines have been reopened to extract the fluorspar and calcite from rocks that were discarded in the past, with lead being extracted from them as a by-product. These operations keep the tradition of lead mining in the Peak District alive.

above In the days when lead mining was a profitable industry, heavy material from within the hillside was placed on wooden chutes to get it outside quickly and efficiently.

CRESWELL CRAGS

19

THE HOME OF ICE AGE ARTISTS

There's no big song and dance heralding your arrival at Creswell Crags. Your approach through a landscape of former mining villages will be guided by a few brown signs pointing the way. Then you end up in a wooded area with a car park next to the visitor centre. There's so much about Creswell Crags that is gloriously understated. It's a visitor attraction that doesn't show off, doesn't pretend to be something it isn't and doesn't create a fuss. It doesn't need to. As home to the most northerly rock art in Europe, Creswell Crags, a former mining community where Derbyshire meets Nottinghamshire, has a unique selling point of global significance that it delivers with perfect modesty and humility. Sign up for one of the cave tours before you arrive and check in at the reception area. Two trips to the caves are available. One shows the engraved cave art that Creswell has become famous for, and the other reveals a more substantial cave that was once home to hyenas, bears and nomadic humans – though obviously not at the same time! Both trips are well worth taking and they're reached by taking a 10-minute walk through the picnic site to an ornamental

THE LOWDOWN

LOCATION Head towards Creswell from M1 junct 30, then follow signs from A616

OPENING HOURS Tours run at weekends (and weekdays in school holidays); can be booked in advance

PRICE £9/£7.50/£6. Children under 5 are not permitted for safety reasons

TEL 01909 720378
EMAIL info@cres well-crags.org.uk
WEBSITE www.cres well-crags.org.uk

ADDRESS Crags Road, Creswell, Worksop, S80 3LH

lake. This stretch of water was built by the Victorian landowner in an attempt to defy railway companies that wanted to build a line through the middle of the crags.

During your visit, make sure you build in enough time to visit the small exhibition that's included in your cave tour ticket. This is a wonderful collection of significant historical artefacts, and it's presented in a simple, effective manner. By not going overboard on the number of exhibits on show and providing a clear explanation of what you do see, Creswell Crags delivers one of the country's best on-site historical displays. There are remains of animals such as bears, hyenas, lions, reindeer and rhino in the exhibition – all of them found in and around the local caves and providing evidence of the changing climate over tens of thousands of years. And although Creswell Crags has become well known for its cave art, there are also examples of ancient portable art in the visitor centre, in the form of carefully crafted images of animals and humans etched onto pieces of bone thousands of years ago.

Deciding on which tour to opt for determines which county you walk into. The lake marks the boundary, putting the rock art cave in Nottinghamshire and the Robin Hood Cave in Derbyshire. The latter gives more underground exploring and you'll have to crouch down through a small passage before getting to the larger cavern, which opens up all around you. It's incredible to think that our ancestors once took shelter in here, lit fires and cooked food. They would probably not have spent lengthy amounts of time in it, though, given that that they didn't have any means of lighting it and there is no natural ventilation for the smoke to leave. But remains of tools and bones found in

A limestone gorge featuring caves and smaller fissures used by prehistoric people and creatures

Animal remains and stone tools have been found and dated back to the last Ice Age

The only cave in Britain known to house Ice Age rock art

opposite The caves within Creswell Crags are only accessible to those explorers who book themselves a place on the tour.

below As well as humans, the caves were also home to bears and lions.

this cavern show that it was once inhabited – and not just by humans. A bear skeleton was discovered huddled in the corner of the cave and the remains of several hyenas were also found in this underground lair.

A gap leading through to another section of the Robin Hood Cave is sealed off. You can peer inside, but you are unlikely to see the inhabitants who currently dwell in there. For this protected area is a bat cave – home to a colony of these winged mammals that fly in and out of their underground accommodation each night. From the main section of the cave, you can see a passage outside with daylight streaming through, and this forms the route that the bats take. On several occasions during the summer, bat experts come to Creswell Crags and lead viewing tours. Monitoring also takes place to estimate just how many bats are living in the dark corners of Robin Hood Cave.

GOING DEEPER...

When the last Ice Age encroached on Britain and transformed the landscape into a snowy wilderness, the area around Creswell Crags was about as far north as humans could survive. At the height of the icy conditions, nobody could tolerate the Creswell climate all year round, but there were a few weeks in the summer when groups of nomadic humans would arrive here and take shelter in the caves. They hunted animals and cooked their meat, using tools made of stone, bone and ivory that have been discovered in the caves at Creswell Crags.

above The country's only prehistoric rock art stayed hidden until 2003.

One of the most significant discoveries at the site came in 2003 when researchers explored the caves at Creswell as well as in other parts the UK, scrutinising them for cave art dating back to the last Ice Age. While studies at other sites failed to reveal anything at the time, there was much excitement when 13,000-year-old cave drawings were found in Church Hole Cave at Creswell Crags. It was a hugely important discovery – the first of its kind in Britain, and one of international importance, for these are the world's most northerly examples of cave art, and include engraved figures of birds, deer and bison. It was an incredible find, linking the humans living in caves on the

Derbyshire border with groups living elsewhere across Europe where similar cave drawings have also been found. Booking for the rock art cave tours is recommended because they are extremely popular. People come from all over the country to climb the steps to the Church Hole Cave and see the fascinating cave art for themselves.

In view of the significance of the contents of Creswell Crags, this is now one of the most heavily protected sites in the country. As well as being a Site of Special Scientific Interest, the crags also benefit from being a Scheduled Ancient Monument and an Area of Local Landscape Significance. The longer-term aim, however, is to secure World Heritage status for Creswell Crags, putting them on a global footing with other significant historical sites around the world. A previous attempt in the 1980s was unsuccessful, but the discovery of Ice Age cave art, portable art on pieces of bone and a variety of tools has added to the crags' worldwide significance.

THE SOUTHEAST

CENTURIES OF CONFLICT between
Britain and its neighbours in Europe have
left a legacy of hideaways in the southeast
of England. From these secret locations
beneath the surface, battle strategies were
drawn up and survival plans evaluated.
Tunnelling into the white cliffs of Dover
initially housed soldiers preparing for battle
with Napoleon. They were later adapted to
provide hospital care for injured troops in
World War II and became the headquarters
for Operation Dynamo as over 300,000
soldiers were evacuated across the Channel
from Dunkirk. The heart of the British war
effort beat fiercely underground in London
at Churchill's War Rooms, where the famous
Map Room and living quarters used by
the Prime Minister are incredibly well
preserved. In Ramsgate, an ambitious plan
allowed the entire town to shelter from Nazi
bombing raids and gave many homeless
families a permanent subterranean address
during the war years. A war refuge of a
more chilling sort is accessible at Kelvedon
Hatch Bunker, a massive complex below
Essex that would have housed Margaret
Thatcher's government in the event of
a nuclear attack during the 1980s.

right A telephone exchange in tunnels deep inside
Dover's white cliffs was important during the war
effort and the underground complex was often
visited by Winston Churchill.

GRIME'S GRAVES

02

A HISTORIC SITE MINED FOR A MILLENNIUM

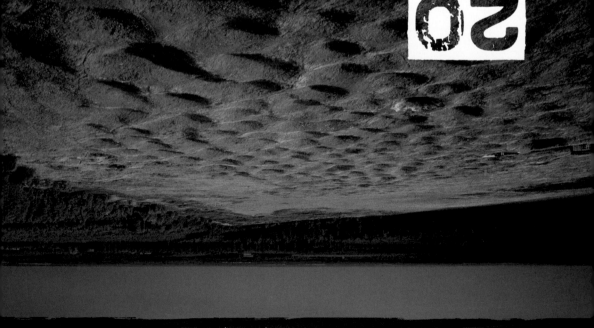

When the Anglo-Saxons arrived here and discovered this large, pockmarked landscape, they presumed it was the work of a deity. Looking so evocative and profound, they thought the land had been crafted by the pagan god Grim – also known as Woden – so they gave his name to the site. Even today, Grime's Graves remains an other-worldly vision, especially when seen from above. When you arrive, following in the footsteps of so many others down the centuries, try to time your visit with one of the tours organised by English Heritage. This will allow you to learn much more about the site at the hands of an expert. Details and dates of the different tours, including family events, are updated on the website.

It's difficult to get a feel for the highly unusual, undulating landscape from the ground. If you stand on a highpoint that gives you a bit of elevation, you'll be able to see a few of the hollows that surround you. For the full effect, look at one of the postcards in the shop or at the image on the front of the English Heritage guidebook. The dips and humps that make this site so special spread out before your eyes. You can walk

THE LOWDOWN

LOCATION The site is signed off the A134 between Thetford and Mundford

OPENING HOURS 1 Apr to 30 Sept 10–6; Oct 10–5; closed Nov–Mar

ADDRESS Grime's Graves – Prehistoric Flint Mine, Lynford, Thetford, Norfolk, IP26 5DE

PRICE £4.60/£4.10/£2.80 family £12. Free for members

TEL 01842 810656

WEBSITE www.english-heritage.co.uk

along the paths that weave in and out of them. These hollows are the visible remains of the pits and mining shafts. There are a remarkable 433 of them to be seen today. Excavation of the site started in 1852, but only 28 have been properly explored. These fascinating earthworks cover over seven hectares and radar surveys have highlighted many other shafts on the same site.

In 1915, to help aid the excavations that were taking place, the mines were given numbers. Pit 1 is open to the public, and by descending a 9m ladder you can get up close to the galleries worked by Neolithic miners. Access is found to the rear of the shop, only becoming visible as you get close to it because the small building that provides access is built in one of the hollows. There'll be a guide in there to help you get kitted out with a hard hat and make sure the journey down the ladder and back up again is safe. It's quite a small space down there in the mine and so the number of visitors at any one time is restricted. But you won't be rushed, and you'll have a good opportunity to explore the mine.

After glancing down the shaft into the dark, it's time to step

Infilled prehistoric pits and shafts have left a surreal, undulating landscape

The only place in Britain to see where Neolithic miners worked

Located on an important area of chalk grassland that is home to many plants and animals

opposite The scarred landscape is a truly surreal landscape when seen from above.

below A few steps down the ladder takes you back over 4,000 years.

onto the ladder and begin the descent. The journey down goes on for longer than you imagine it might, but eventually your feet reach the chalky surface at the bottom of the ladder. There are lights on down here, so you can peer from the bottom of the shaft into the galleries that were opened up. From here, crouch down and imagine Neolithic miners using antlers as tools to pick off the flint deposits from the rock. The direction these galleries were worked followed the line of flint. Some of them are more than 15m long and link up with other shafts. These Neolithic mines you are wandering around first started to be worked around 2650 BC – around when Stonehenge was being erected. But despite the high number of shafts, this was never an area of intensive mining. Over a period of 1,100 years, it's thought that the Grime's Graves site contained between 500 and 1,000 shafts and pits. It is therefore likely that only one or two of the flint mines were active at any given time.

It's fairly cool at the bottom of the shaft, and on a warm day you'll really feel the heat hit you when you arrive back at the top of the ladder. During your visit here, make time to take a walk on the paths that criss-cross over the chalky grasslands. In the summer months, there are many flowers growing here that add to the charm. There are also adders living in the longer grass, so make sure you stick to the well-trodden route and avoid the longer grass.

below Workings go off in different directions and link up with the other mines.

GOING DEEPER...

It's not just flint mining that has been important at Grime's Graves. When the Anglo-Saxons arrived here and thought the dented fields were the work of the god Grim, they assumed the hill to the east of the site was his burial mound. This peak is now known as Grimshoe Mound. The word "hoe" means burial mound, reflecting their belief that the hill was the final resting place of Grim. So significant was Grimshoe Mound that local leaders held meetings on top of the hill to settle any disputes that arose.

Excavations in the 1970s discovered that the Grime's Graves site was also used as a place to bury the dead. Approximately 1,000 years after the flint mines were last used, Iron Age dwellers held ceremonies here to inter people. One young adult woman was discovered buried in the upper part of a shaft that had been filled, and sloe was discovered near the place an adult man had been buried. Next to him, two iron beads were found that are thought to be from a necklace or other form of jewellery.

In more recent history, there is a *Dad's Army*-style story to be told about Grime's Graves. During World War II, because this area was one of the few open clearings to be found in Thetford Forest, there was a real concern that it could be the focus of a German invasion. A particular worry was that gliders carrying troops could fly over and parachute soldiers directly into the clearing. To combat the threat, the Home Guard dug down to create a series of foxholes. Each one could hold one man in a shelter just over half a metre deep. The plan was that in an emergency, the Home Guard would be able to attack the invading soldiers from the foxholes, a group of which can be seen in the ground between the car park and the visitor centre. Another group can still be seen over on the eastern edge of the site – close to where the Anglo-Saxons had staged their important meetings on Grimshoe Mound thousands of years earlier.

above The huge site has been the scene of burials and worship as well as mining.

KELVEDON HATCH SECRET NUCLEAR BUNKER

21

WHEN TWO TRIBES GO TO WAR

Following a road sign for a 'secret' nuclear bunker in Essex seems riddled with irony. The large brown tourist sign openly points the way to this unusual and quite remarkable attraction, encouraging visitors to delve into some Cold War history. But in the 1980s, when the threat of nuclear war was very real, this was indeed a truly secret bunker. Only a select number of people knew it was there, waiting to be used if the horrors of nuclear war became a reality. Being located so close to London, this underground bunker would likely be the place where senior government and military officials would take shelter and try to run the country as best they could in the aftermath of a nuclear attack. It's possible the Prime Minister of the day, Margaret Thatcher, would have been brought here.

The entrance to the bunker is quite a way from the road. The first hint that you are drawing near comes when you see the large transmitter on top

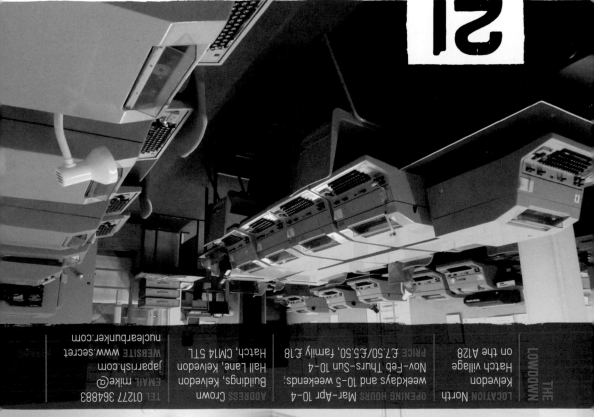

THE LOWDOWN

LOCATION North Kelvedon Hatch village on the A128

OPENING HOURS Mar–Apr 10–4 weekdays and 10–5 weekends; Nov–Feb Thurs–Sun 10–4

PRICE £7.50/£5.50, family £18

ADDRESS Crown Buildings, Kelvedon Hall Lane, Kelvedon Hatch, CM14 5TL

TEL 01277 364883

EMAIL mike@japarrish.com

WEBSITE www.secret nuclearbunker.com

of the hill. This is the only evidence of the bunker's existence that can be seen from the surrounding area. After parking up, follow the signs for the entrance down a little dip and through some woodland. The small bungalow you come to looks unremarkable, just like a secluded house, and certainly nothing to indicate what's beneath it. But at the back of this building a long tunnel takes you into the hill towards two large blast doors and, beyond those, inside the top-secret Cold War hideout.

Your entrance into this bunker today could not be more different from the high security that once enveloped it. On a quiet day it's possible that you won't see any members of staff there. Instead, instructions on a sign at the entrance ask you to proceed into the tunnel and pay at the end. You're told to collect an audio guide and then you begin self-touring around the facility, following arrows on the floor. When you're finished, you enter the canteen at the end of the tour and are asked to put money into an honesty box. Credit and debit cards are not accepted at the bunker.

Until you step foot inside it and see it for yourself, it's hard to comprehend that this bunker was actually planned and built. Some of the rooms you visit on your way around the mesmerising space are mind-blowing. The recording booth, complete with BBC microphones and now including a model of Margaret Thatcher making a statement to the nation, would have been one of the most important. It was from here that the radio broadcasts would have been made to let people know what was going on, what to do, how to behave and what was being done to help.

The sick bay has the familiar smell of a hospital and was equipped to deal with a range of injuries and illnesses. Peer into the dormitories to get a feel for how many people would have stayed here and the nature of their cramped conditions. You'll pass some of the large

Designed to be the regional base of the British government following a nuclear attack

Three floors of subterranean accommodation and communication and catering facilities

Cleverly disguised as a bungalow at the surface

opposite Kelvedon was capable of housing a significant administration.

below A transmission mast gave the only clue to the bunker's location.

machinery in the bunker, designed to blast out waste, keep the conditions cool and filter the air being brought in. And dwell a while in what would have been the operations room to study the maps, plotting where nuclear blasts had taken place and where fallout was expected. If you're feeling energetic, you can arrange for your visit to include an attempt to master the high ropes course just outside the nuclear bunker. Visit the website and see the link for Rope Runners for details about how to book.

Provisions were stockpiled in the bunker to allow the selected staff to stay there for three months following a nuclear attack. After that, they could no longer be fully protected from what was happening on the surface. In those three months, the outside world would have changed beyond recognition.

GOING DEEPER...

Walking around the secret nuclear bunker at Kelvedon Hatch is an eerie experience. For those who were alive during the 1980s, it will bring back memories about the very real threat of nuclear war that existed back then. One of the more startling aspects of a visit here lies in the opportunity it provides to learn about the preparations that were made for an attack from Russia. Many civilians at the time thought it was inevitable that entire cities would be wiped out in an organised nuclear attack, and when you discover the serious planning that the leaders of the country back then put into preparing for nuclear war, it's clear that those fears were well founded.

right Rockets are displayed there today but originally the entrance was designed to look like a normal house.

The government of the day was preparing for a 'period of tension' when diplomatic relations between East and West would be almost at breaking point. At this time, a series of information films would be played frequently on television so that families could prepare for war. These films are available to watch within the Kelvedon Hatch Secret Nuclear Bunker, and it's alarming to imagine the population of the UK having to take it all in and wait for the worst. People would have been given information about the blast and about fallout threats from the bomb. They were to be educated about the different sirens and sounds that would tell them that a nuclear attack was imminent and that radioactive fallout was due. A cartoon playing to visitors to the bunker explains the

above With the bunker running on its own power supply, the government of the day would have attempted to keep order from here.

damage that a nuclear attack could cause to houses. It's chilling to watch it today, but those films would have terrified people in the 1980s if they had been shown in earnest. They would probably have led to mass panic. Another video you'll be able to watch shows a man emerge from his household's nuclear shelter and examine all his rooms to check for damage. The films are naïve and simple, aimed at reassuring people before the attack. Just how much help they would have given in the event of an actual attack is debatable.

As the population as a whole became obsessed with the prospect of nuclear war, so too did popular culture. Topping the pop charts, Frankie Goes to Hollywood's 'Two Tribes' explored the prospect of war. The various versions and mixes featured sirens and government-style instructions about what to do. The sleeve to the very popular 12-inch mix showed the effects of a nuclear winter. Raymond Briggs, who drew *The Snowman* book, delivered a disturbing cartoon called *When the Wind Blows* that showed an elderly couple dealing with a nuclear attack and dying of radiation sickness. It scared schoolchildren up and down the country with its realism. And the TV programme *Threads*, written by Barry Hines and showing the impact of war in Sheffield, was a gritty and disturbing examination of nuclear war. Spending time beforehand exploring these works of art will enhance your trip to the bunker.

CHURCHILL WAR ROOMS 2

FROM DARKEST HOUR TO FINEST HOUR

Chosen because of its proximity to the Houses of Parliament and Downing Street, this large basement on King Charles Street allowed the government to stay safely in the centre of London during World War II. One other option being considered in the late 1930s was to evacuate key government members to the suburbs and possibly to the West Country in order to keep them safe from aerial bombardment. But keeping the Prime Minister in the heart of the city was of extreme symbolic importance, and was a means of keeping the nation on the government's side. Housing the Cabinet in the King Charles Street basement was thus a crucial decision and one that boosted the morale of troops, politicians and civilians alike. This location, within earshot of Big Ben, was ideal. Work began on transforming the space beneath the New Public Offices during the summer of 1938 in anticipation of conflict. Sandbags were put in place, rooms emptied, brick partitions built and glass doors replaced. Airlocks were fitted to guard against gas attacks, and commu-nication lines were installed so that the Prime Minister could broadcast to the nation via the BBC.

Much of the story of World War II unfolded in the city of London. This is where Churchill stoically planned the nation's response to the Nazi aggressors. Several areas of London bore the brunt of the Blitz as a new era of air warfare arrived. When you descend the steps and head into the basement of the government offices in Whitehall, you can almost taste the history. These underground corridors of power have a story to tell at every corner, and the impeccable way in which everything has been preserved from those dark days in the early 1940s is phenomenal. After getting your tickets, the most important job is to pick up an audio guide. These come with a range of languages pre-installed, and there is also a version with a more child-friendly narrative. Staff at the War Rooms will set the guide to your requirements and then you're off on a self-guided journey around the World War II command centre. Try to stop at as many of the numbered audio-guide stops as possible. Whenever you punch in the number and listen to the description for that particular place, you receive a fascinating explanation of what happened on that spot during the war years.

All the rooms in this network of corridors beneath the capital are important in their own right. One, though, has a very special significance in the history of the nation. The map

left Churchill sent a strong message when choosing to locate his headquarters in the heart of London.

previous page Walk along corridors once trod by Churchill and the team who masterminded the war effort.

22 CHURCHILL WAR ROOMS

room was the beating heart of the Cabinet War Rooms. This place brought together all the intelligence that had been gathered from around the world. The team of 'plotters' then added labels to the many maps mounted on the walls. A week before the war broke out, the team assigned to this room moved in and switched on the strip lights. They would not be turned off until the end of the war, for throughout the war years, this room was used around the clock. Close by, a small store room off the main corridor had a new door fitted in 1943, with what looked like a lavatory-style lock. Rumours began to circulate about Churchill having his own private toilet there, but the truth was far more interesting. It housed the first hotline between London and Washington, allowing Churchill to speak to President Roosevelt secretly through a secure telephone link.

Incorporated within the Churchill War Rooms is the Churchill Museum. Entry is included with your ticket. The museum, occupying further areas of the basement, gives a very detailed and at times candid insight into the life of one of the world's most famous leaders. Within the Churchill Museum, you can learn more about the man himself through a series

below Beneath the bustling streets of the capital, the famous Map Room saw major wartime decisions taken.

of displays about his life before, during and after the war. But the real feature here – the exhibit you could spend literally hours exploring – is the Churchill Lifeline. Dominating the centre of the room, the lengthy interactive table with a touch-screen surface lets you examine a wealth of information about Churchill in chronological order. Simply choose a date and you'll find out what Churchill was up to in what is essentially an interactive diary. With thousands of documents, photographs, animations and short films all available within the Churchill Lifeline, it's the part of the experience many history buffs become lost in. There are so many different avenues to explore, every visitor will leave with a different titbit of information on Churchill, from his obsession with taking hot baths to the amount of work he completed in bed.

above Much of Churchill's labour in the war was carried out in bed, which he valued as a constructive work space.

GOING DEEPER...

When Hitler rose to power in 1933 and announced that Germany was leaving the League of Nations, governments across Europe started to realise that another conflict could be on the cards. Little more than a decade after World War I, national defence was once again given top priority in Britain. Security chiefs knew the next conflict would be different, involving thousands of bombs being dropped from the sky.

A safe haven was needed for key members of the government, and it had to have the protection of being underground. When Germany annexed Austria in 1938, the search was stepped up for a subterranean location within the capital city.

The War Rooms were ready to be used by September 1938, but had they been needed immediately it would not have been a comfortable existence. The ventilation system was poor, there was nowhere to sleep and facilities for cooking and washing were non-existent. At that time, the toilets took the shape of a row of buckets. More work was needed to convert the War Rooms completely, and thankfully the 'peace in our time' Munich Agreement bought some time. At the end of August 1939 this complex was officially opened – and that turned out to be just in time. Less than a week later, Germany invaded Poland. Two days after that, Britain was at war with Germany.

below The warren of passages below London is now also home to the Churchill Museum and a themed tea room.

Neville Chamberlain was Prime Minister when war was declared, though no meetings were held in the Central War Room until the end of October 1939, because the immediate bombing of London that had been expected did not take place. But after a poor land campaign in Norway and with Germany on the advance in the Low Countries, Chamberlain's days as leader came to an end. He resigned on 10 May 1940, and Winston Churchill was confirmed as the new Prime Minister on the same day. During the Blitz, Churchill made radio addresses to the nation from the War Rooms, while more and more staff slept down there to avoid the falling bombs. The nine-month-long Blitz took a heavy toll on the city of London, but the War Rooms remained intact. The closest heavy explosion left a crater near Clive Steps, close to where you enter the War Rooms as a visitor.

Three years after the war, the incredibly well-preserved rooms were declared a monument. During the 1950s, '60s and '70s, free guided tours of the War Rooms were available to people who had written to the Cabinet Office and asked to see them. The Imperial War Museum gained permission to turn the War Rooms into an official museum in the early 1980s, with the first of its millions of visitors queuing up to experience this underground headquarters in 1984.

23 MAIL RAIL AT THE POSTAL MUSEUM

A FIRST CLASS PASSAGE

Opened in 2017, the Postal Museum and its underground Mail Rail relay the history of communication over the last 500 years, from some of the first letters ever sent by mail to the introduction of the postage stamp, and from telegrams sent using Morse Code to the red telephone boxes that have come to symbolise the nation. You'll see a mail carriage that carried post under lock and key and had armed guards on board to deter highwaymen. There's a chance to examine the methods used to pick up and drop off bags of mail from speeding trains that contained their own sorting office. You don't need to be a communication geek or a stamp collector to enjoy a visit to the Postal Museum; there's plenty to interest anybody wanting a better understanding of the world's most famous mail network.

Even though the main site on Phoenix Place has the café, one of the early green post boxes and information about *Star Wars* stamps, the main attraction

Home of the Mail Rail – an underground train network at the heart of British communications for 75 years

The Postal Museum tells the story of written communication over the last 500 years

Various mail-related events, talks and walking tours can be booked through the museum's website

– the Mail Rail – is across the road beneath the existing Royal Mail depot. Tickets for the Mail Rail need to be ordered online in advance if you want to guarantee your underground journey. The Mail Rail trains leave every few minutes, and the advance ticket will give you a 20-minute time slot in which to arrive. This is a popular activity in London and the number of seats is limited for each train, so tickets sell out on many days – especially weekends and holidays.

It's better to explore the Postal Museum before you embark on your Mail Rail journey. The exhibits in the museum deal with many features of the postal service before work started on the underground network in 1915. It's good to get a feel for these early years of the postal delivery service before moving across the road for a more modern experience. Those first decades are a stark contrast to the underground rails that dominated the distribution of the capital's post throughout most of the 20th century.

As you enter the Mail Rail building, you'll descend into the old Mount Pleasant underground postal station. This was once the beating heart of the Mail Rail, with a busy sorting office above ground linked to trains that left the platforms every four minutes. It was part of a 10km underground network that had eight separate stations and linked the city's mail hubs with major train stations such as Liverpool Street and Paddington. From here, letters were distributed around the country. Take time to view the films on display in this huge space before joining the queue for your train. They are very informative presentations, showing pictures of the underground mail network in operation down here, and including quotes from people who carried out what was often gruelling work.

The Mail Rail is an actual train that used to carry bags of mail beneath the streets of London. It's much smaller than a normal train, so it can be a tight squeeze for passengers. There are a number of restrictions and requirements that mean the short journey isn't for everybody. Riders must be able to climb the 70 steps to the surface, walk unaided on uneven surfaces and be comfortable in confined spaces. Visitors who don't fancy boarding the little train can enjoy a film of the journey on a screen close to the departing platform.

previous page The nation's mail used to pass through the capital along a secret underground rail network.

Each compartment in the carriage has room for a couple of people. The views from the train are great thanks to an innovative redesign that added a see-through roof, allowing you to look at everything on both sides. This all-round view is really put to good use at the two stations you pull into, where short videos are projected onto the white walls, telling the story of what happened in this workplace between World War I and the closure of the line in 2003. Combined with the audio guide that accompanies the journey, it's an effective multi-media approach to the trip.

The Mail Rail takes passengers on a small loop to show the hidden tunnels and stations that were once so important in getting correspondence to the right parts of the country. You're brought back to the same station and then have the opportu-

below A new addition to the Postal Museum – visitors can book in for a journey on Mail Rail.

nity to explore an exhibition about the history of trains and their links with the postal service. Don't miss the chance to sort letters into the correct pigeonholes in a replica train – complete with wobbling floor!

GOING DEEPER...

Many years before work started on Mail Rail, the Victorians kept the capital's post on the move by creating a series of tunnels three metres below the city's busy streets. Opened in February 1863, the system saw parcels and letters carried between Euston Station and nearby Eversholt Street in subterranean cars. Powered by a fan, they ran on rails and delivered the post until they were shelved in 1866. Although these vehicles were briefly reintroduced in the 1870s, they were not a long-term solution to the problem of delivering mail efficiently in a busy capital city.

Congestion on London's streets got worse as the city moved into the 20th century. By 1909, mail was being transported above ground at an average speed of just seven miles an hour. The Post Office controller, Robert Bruce, knew something had to be done and proposed a new underground train network that would sit 20m below the surface. Work started on digging the secret tunnels in 1914, following a carefully planned route. Construction work was delayed during World War I, but the two-foot-gauge railway was finally opened in 1927 and operated continuously until 2003, by which time it was no longer considered to be cost effective.

When you ride the Mail Rail – originally known by the less snappy name 'Post Office (London) Railway' – there will be a driver in charge of your train. The original vehicles carrying the city's mail, however, were driverless. Controlled remotely, these electric trains travelled at 30mph and inclines were built at the stations to help them slow down. Throughout the working life of the Mail Rail, some 180 different mail cars were used. They each averaged eight metres in length and were made of four sections that carried as many as 21 bags of mail. It was the job of workers on the platforms to quickly load and unload the bags in the short time that the trains were stopped. The trains were maintained by a team of engineers who worked hard to ensure there were very few delays on the Mail Rail network.

> The original vehicles carrying the city's mail were driverless. Controlled remotely, these electric trains travelled at 30mph and inclines were built at the stations to help them slow down.

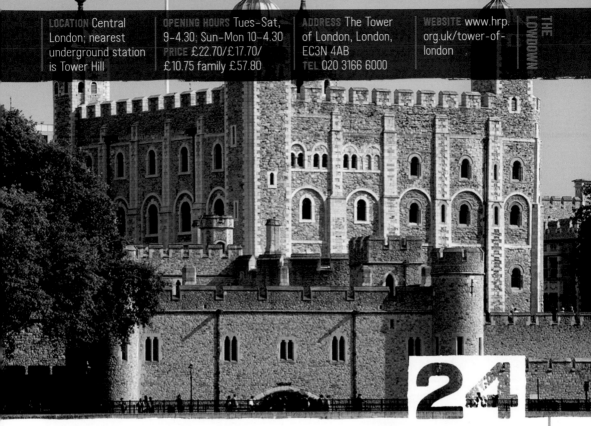

24

WAKEFIELD TOWER (TOWER OF LONDON)

SEND THEM TO THE TOWER

Forget some of the modern, re-created dungeon experiences you can have – a journey into the basement of Wakefield Tower brings you up close with just how savage people could be in days gone by. There's no attempt at all to play on the gruesome nature of the torture instruments and there's no added gore to sensationalise your brief visit to this small room. In fact, the exhibition itself is very simple. There are three replica instruments of torture and a written explanation describing how each was used. It's chillingly effective. These are horrendous inventions designed to inflict excruciating pain and they were really used on humans. Given the nature of what's in here, leaving some things to the imagination can add its own sense of horror. And it might not be everybody's cup of tea. It's certainly less cheery than the Crown Jewels experience nearby. But it's just as big a part of this great castle's incredible history.

In the centre of the room is a replica of the rack,

perhaps the most infamous torture instrument. Prisoners were strapped to this cruel invention and forced into revealing their secrets. The operators turned the handle and caused the victim's body to stretch and contort. Aggressive and determined questioning would have mixed with screams of pain. Several people were broken on the rack at the Tower of London. Anne Askew was one such person, interrogated in the 1540s with the aim of obtaining the names of protestant sympa-

thisers. In her diary, she wrote about being subjected to the rack until nearly dead. When she was sentenced to death, Askew had to be carried to her execution as the torture had left her unable to walk. She was the only person on record to be both tortured in the Tower and burnt at the stake.

Working in the opposite way to the rack, 'the scavenger's daughter' was a torture instrument which compressed bodies instead of stretching them. With the victim kneeling down, the metal constraints held them in place in a dangerously uncomfortable position. With unbearable pain being suffered, this terrible treatment could soon result in their lungs filling with blood. And if you thought things couldn't get any worse, the third instrument is 'the manacles'. With this monster, torturous metal rings were placed over the wrists of the victim, tight enough so that their hands could not be removed from them. They were then forced up a couple of steps, had their hands raised and the manacles placed through an iron bar. When the steps were removed, they were left to hang there. Although these are replica instruments, there are plenty of chilling genuine weapons to see in the nearby armouries.

The basement of the Wakefield Tower is one of the spookiest places to visit in the Tower of London, though it will take up just a fraction of your time here. The Tower is one of the capital's top tourist draws – expect queues and bag searches on your way in – and there's enough to keep you occupied all day. As soon as you're inside you'll see signs for the guided tours given by the Yeomen Warders. These are free, and they set off every 30 minutes, providing detailed information about the chapel, executions, Traitors' Gate and the Bloody Tower, to name but a few of the areas covered. Elsewhere, take a walk along the battlements for some of the most interesting views in London and enter into one of the most protected vaults on the planet to see the Crown Jewels, which have featured in coronations down the centuries. Tucked away and often missed by visitors, the story of the Royal Mint is a fascinating one. All coins used to be made on this site before 1810, and it was a dangerous business. The exhibition has some phenomenal examples of coins from the days of Henry VIII, Charles II and Elizabeth I.

Hundreds of people were detained here, with the register of inmates reading like a *Who's Who* of treachery.

Famous London castle used down the centuries as a fortress, prison and royal palace

Prisoners held here include Anne Boleyn and Guy Fawkes

Torture sessions were carried out in the tower, and replicas of the instruments used are on display

GOING DEEPER...

Built between AD 1220 and 1240, the Wakefield Tower was originally at the side of the river and served as a royal residence for Henry III. The location meant King Henry could arrive by boat and then swiftly walk up into the tower via a private staircase. The main room in the tower would have served as a private audience chamber, and today it has a replica throne in it based on the Coronation Chair at Westminster Abbey.

In recent years, the Tower of London has housed documents and jewels rather than prisoners seen as a threat to national security. Even though the Tower wasn't built as a prison, it is the legends of incarceration and torture that have been best preserved down the centuries. When tourism became popular here during Victorian times, visitors relished macabre tales from the dungeons, and the Tower's sinister history became legendary. Hundreds of people were detained here, with the register of inmates reading like a *Who's Who* of treachery. The second wife of Henry VIII, Anne Boleyn, was accused of adultery and incest in 1536 and imprisoned at the Tower before being one of only seven people to be executed on Tower Green. The young Princess Elizabeth was brought to the Tower in 1554 when her half-sister, Mary I, reckoned she was plotting against her. Later released and placed under house arrest, she eventually returned to the Tower to prepare for her coronation.

Perhaps the most famous inmate of all was a certain Guy Fawkes, whom we still remember on 5 November. In 1605 an anonymous tip-off alerted James I that his life would be in danger during the state opening of Parliament. A search of the building was promptly ordered and there in the cellar, close to 36 barrels of gunpowder, was Fawkes. He was interrogated and very possibly tortured in the Tower of London, holding out for a few days before naming those who had worked with him. All were rounded up and brought to the Tower, where they faced a most gruesome and public death. First, they were dragged by a horse through the streets of London to Westminster. There they were hanged, drawn and quartered, with their body parts being put on display throughout the city as a deterrent to others. A chilling reminder of the torture Guy Fawkes is likely to have endured can be seen in a comparison of his 'before and after' signatures, a copy of which can be seen in Wakefield Tower. The quivering writing just before his execution is that of a broken man.

25 LEEDS CASTLE MAZE AND GROTTO

FACE TO FACE WITH THE GREEN MAN

It's described as 'the loveliest castle in the world', and it's hard to disagree with the Leeds Castle PR team once you've set eyes on the building and its surroundings. For many, this fits the bill of what a traditional castle should look like – magnificent stonework, extensive grounds, turrets fit for a queen and a moat majestically framing it all. It's certainly one of the most photogenic buildings in the country.

The medieval building, though, is just one of the attractions available at Leeds Castle. Families living nearby will be able to make good use of as the extensive playgrounds, which are a very popular feature among younger visitors who may tire of the castle itself after visiting a few regal rooms. There are areas set aside for younger children as well as a more challenging adventure area for older kids, along with places to sit and get a coffee for worn-out adults. An entry ticket allows you to make use of everything available here as often as you like within one year.

Leeds Castle was utilised by Edward I and Henry VIII as well as being enjoyed as a private home by six of England's queens

Tickets include unlimited visits for a year to the castle, maze, grounds and playgrounds

The famous maze contains 2,400 yew trees and is laid out to resemble a crown

Road access to Leeds Castle is really good; the site is well connected and very close to the motorway. This puts it within a two-hour drive of millions of people and, as such, well worth considering as the destination for a day out. You'll more than likely find yourself going back at different times of the year to take part in the various themed events. And, of course, returning so often will also enable you to become an expert in the art of maze completion!

The maze itself is set in a large area close to the playgrounds and manages to captivate young and old alike with its labyrinth of bending avenues and dead ends. One of the best mazes in the country, this is a large puzzle to solve, and the yew tree interior is very well maintained. Sufficiently tall to stop people peering over and cheating, and thick enough to limit the possibility of gaining clues from seeing people in nearby passages, this is a challenging maze which is not easy to solve. Added to the complexity of the maze is its shape. The design takes the physical space of a square, but seen from above, the design is made of distinctive curves and swirls that give

previous page
Delightfully surreal treasures await under the castle's maze.

below The Green Man is extravagantly designed.

it anything but the rigid appearance most mazes display. This innovative design is unique to the maze at Leeds Castle and gives those trying to get out further problems. Of course, this difficulty is part of the attraction; an easy maze wouldn't make for an enjoyable activity. And judging by the way children and adults keep running back to the entrance to have another go, this is a seriously fun thing to do.

With most mazes, the aim is to get to the middle and then make your way to the exit, which is usually found next to the entrance. But the challenge at the Leeds Castle maze is different, as it includes an underground element. When people make their way to the middle of the maze, they disappear down some steps beneath the Kent landscape and leave the above-ground puzzle by entering an underground grotto that has been ornately decorated. Using different lighting techniques and a range of materials that include sea shells, a mysterious world of huge faces and strange creatures has been created, all of which demand closer inspection.

The different events staged all year round comprise one of the biggest pulls at Leeds Castle. Before you plan your visit, it's worth checking out the website to see what events your trip could coincide with. This is especially the case if you have young children, as there are plenty of themed treats they will

below The underground grotto is an unexpected pleasure, rewarding those successful in the maze.

enjoy. A particularly popular time is Christmas, when you can have a go at wreath making, visit reindeer, see Father Christmas and do some shopping at the Christmas market. At other times of the year there is a winter trail to follow, as well as classical concerts, classic car events, spooky goings-on at Halloween and a very popular firework display to mark Bonfire Night. These themed events are done extremely well at Leeds Castle and as a result they are very popular. But while some people may choose to check the calendar to seek out events such as these that they can join in, those wanting a quieter visit should look at the events diary to pick a week when no extra action is planned.

GOING DEEPER...

Records exist of mazes and labyrinths built for pleasure dating back thousands of years, and there are examples of them being developed in ancient Egypt. The maze at Leeds Castle, however, has much more recent roots. This walkable puzzle was designed in 1987 and has 2,400 yew trees forming the passageways, all of which need regularly looking after. It is one of the trickiest of its kind to solve because of the troublesome shape that misleads people once they're inside, and the average time people spend in there is around 20 minutes. Be

below Rocks and shells used to create folk figures have a startling impact.

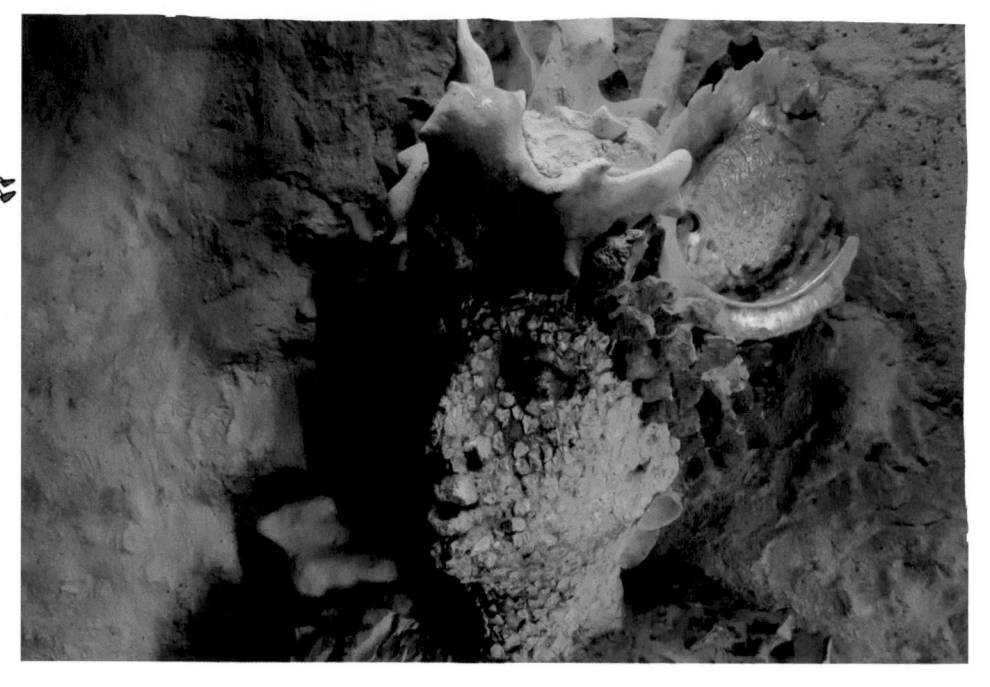

sure to time your own journey inside Leeds Castle maze to see if you're faster than most people at tackling this teaser.

When you've reached the middle of the maze, of course, your underground trip to the grotto begins. Greeting you before you enter this mysterious space is the word 'Metamorphoses'. You'll see it carved into the rock above the entrance. As well as signalling the change of scenery you're about to experience, this is the name of a Roman poem. The story in this historic piece of literature concerns a journey of change amid a backdrop of famous mythological figures. The first of these you come across when you enter the grotto is Typhoeus, a fearsome monster that had a hundred heads and fire bursting from its terrifying eyes. Elsewhere, there are representations of the four elements. These female forms of Earth, Wind, Fire and Water are beautifully decorated, and each deserves your time to gaze at it and take photographs. Continue through an arch of bones towards an awe-inspiring work of art that is a massive phoenix made from shells. Don't forget to look out for Hermit's Cave on the way out, where you'll see a remarkable Green Man if you peer inside. There's plenty of artistic splendour to savour beneath the Leeds Castle maze, and the reaction from most people is that they want to have another go and pass through this amazingly artistic space once more.

25 LEEDS CASTLE MAZE AND GROTTO

RAMSGATE TUNNELS

26

THE TUNNEL THAT SAVED A TOWN

Even on a sunny day in summer, it can be difficult to imagine the hustle and bustle of Ramsgate in its heyday as a popular seaside destination. In the late 19th and early 20th centuries, the beach was regularly packed with thousands of holiday-makers and the harbour train station was a major focal point as many visitors arrived by rail. Day-trippers were transported down to sea level through a cliff-face tunnel and conveniently emerged near the beach. Today, the entrance to the tunnel is remarkably recognisable in old photographs of Ramsgate in its popular past. There's now a car park right next to the entrance, on what used to be the railway sidings, but the charges are expensive. If you can manage the steep, colourful stairs that link the seafront with the clifftop, you may be able to find free roadside parking on the streets above the tunnel.

Two historic uses of the tunnel will be of interest to those visiting, and both are well-covered on the tunnel tour. Its first use, and the reason the space was dug out, was to link the railway with the harbour. The tunnel had a hugely posi-tive impact on the tourist industry and on the whole of the

THE LOWDOWN

LOCATION The Ramsgate sea front, signed from the town centre

OPENING HOURS Apr–Sept, tours at 10, 12, 2 and 4; Oct–Mar, tours at 10, 12 and 2; closed Mon and Tues **PRICE** £7/£5/£4

ADDRESS Ramsgate Tunnels, Marina Esplanade, Ramsgate, Kent, CT11 8FH

TEL 01843 588123 **EMAIL** admin@ramsgatetunnels.org **WEBSITE** www.ramsgatetunnels.org

town's economy for decades. But the majority of your visit will be spent exploring and learning about the 2.5-mile labyrinth of wartime shelters that connects with the old railway tunnel and that was created in the late 1930s as the threat of war loomed in Europe. To add to the atmosphere, the entrance to the tunnel is charmingly decorated in a World War II theme. Music from the time helps to take your mind back to this difficult period, and you can enjoy a snack in a 1940s-style café.

Railway tunnel dating back to 1863, initially serving Ramsgate Harbour Station

Network of underground war shelters developed during the build up to World War II

Became permanent underground settlement for homeless victims of the Blitz

While there may have been a heightened sense of community during the bombing raids of World War II and stories of helping out neighbours are commonplace, these were extremely tough times for families. Watching the old black-and-white news reel before the tour begins will give you an idea of how testing an era it was for the town's population. Heading underground night after night to escape the potential fury of passing enemy planes, people emerged hours later to discover whether their house was still standing. Hundreds became permanent residents in this underground settlement, setting up beds in the main railway tunnel and putting up makeshift

opposite Hundreds of families were housed in subterranean Ramsgate. Today's visitors can see what their shelters would have been like.

below When the lights come on, the full extent of the tunnels is revealed.

partitions to create a modicum of privacy. Some reconstructed family areas show the cramped conditions that many people lived in during this time. Rowdy underground parties had to be restricted to a couple of nights a week so that people could get a little sleep before starting work the next day.

The tour begins in the railway tunnel and, in a real 'wow' moment, introduces the wartime shelters by turning on the lights to reveal a lengthy chalk passageway stretching off as far as you can see into the distance. Heading down here, you'll be told a wealth of stories about what happened beneath

Ramsgate during the war and about how some groups used to come in and explore the tunnel network in the 1970s. One fantastic link with the past is the extensive graffiti that can be seen drawn on the chalk walls. From people's initials to flags and children's games, all were etched by anxious fingers on the chalk and give a fascinating insight into those troubled years.

People made the decision to set up long-term homes in the main tunnel for various reasons. Maybe their house had been destroyed, or maybe they were extremely fearful of what was to come. Although the conditions in the subterranean shelter were far from palatial, this was a popular place because it was safe. And the decision to go ahead with this controversial shelter was justified on Saturday 24 August 1940, which turned out to be Ramsgate's worst day of the war. At the time, the aerial assault on the town was the worst ever experienced. The leading aircraft in the raid was shot down as it approached Ramsgate, prompting the rest of the pilots to drop their entire load onto the town and return to Germany. In total, the German planes dropped 500 bombs onto the coastal town in five minutes, killing 29 civilians and two soldiers as well as damaging 1,200 homes. Experts agree that the death toll would have been much higher if it hadn't been for the underground tunnel network that could hold up to 60,000 people – more than the population of Ramsgate at the time. There was room down here for everyone living nearby, and without it the toll of the war in the Southeast would surely have been far higher.

> The death toll would have been much higher if it hadn't been for the underground tunnel network that could hold up to 60,000 people – more than the population of Ramsgate at the time.

GOING DEEPER...

The tunnels at Ramsgate are now famous for their role in World War II, but back in 1863, when it started out as a railway tunnel, the underground system had also played a crucial role in the town's development. The Ramsgate Harbour Station was accessed by the tunnel, which linked with London and allowed goods to be brought to and from ships bound for or coming from Ostend. The tunnel was abandoned in 1926 when a new station was built in Ramsgate, though a light was shone on it once again ten years later in 1936, when an electric railway was developed to link the train station with the beach and the 'Merrie England' amusement area. It featured a five-minute journey through the tunnel, with illuminated scenes

from around the world on display along the route. The tunnel became a tourist attraction in its own right and remained popular until it was closed in the 1960s. When you visit, look out for the large letters that lean against the wall of the tunnel. Originally spelling out 'Tunnel Railway', they are now a rusty reminder of Ramsgate's past as a bustling seaside resort.

As tensions built across Europe in the 1930s, plans to extend the tunnel system and use it as a huge air-raid shelter began to take shape. The towns along the Kent coast had already been introduced to the horror of aerial bombing raids during World War I. People knew that if another war broke out with Germany, the bombardment from the air would be a lot worse. When the Germans occupied Austria in 1938, a council plan for the shelters was presented to the government, but funding was not approved. It was only on the third time of asking, in March 1939, that the Home Office gave permission to build the tunnels. Work started on digging out the country's largest wartime shelter soon after. The first section of the Ramsgate Tunnels, linking the Harbour East entrance with Queen Street, was opened on 1 June 1939 by the Duke of Kent. Three months later, Germany invaded Poland and war was declared by Prime Minister Neville Chamberlain. The persistence of Ramsgate's mayor in the late 1930s had played a pivotal role in getting the town's air-raid shelters developed. Some referred to ABC Kempe as the 'Mad Mayor', but thanks to him hundreds of lives were saved when the bombs started to fall on Ramsgate.

above The tunnels were closed off during the war, seen only by adventurous trespassers in the 1970s.

27

DOVER CASTLE WORLD WAR II TUNNELS

HUGE ACHIEVEMENT OF THE LITTLE SHIPS

The medieval fortress standing high above the strategic stronghold of Dover dates back to the 11th century. Prized by generations of kings and queens, Dover Castle has a formidable position gazing out towards France, and it played a major role in many conflicts. During World War II, the castle survived Germany's aerial bombardment, despite much of the nearby town being flattened and the region being nicknamed Hellfire Corner. The labyrinth of tunnels beneath the castle dates back to Napoleonic days, but the tunnels had their greatest hour as the headquarters for Operation Dynamo, when the evacuation of Dunkirk was planned and executed in 1940.

There are two underground tours to go on, both included in the general admission fee to Dover Castle. The two tunnels involved occupy different levels within the white cliffs. They are essentially on top of each other, separated by a few metres of rock.

A third tunnel complex was dug as a Cold War bunker, but this is not open to the public.

The entrances to both tunnels are close to each other and well signed within the castle grounds. If you plan on visiting both, experience the Dunkirk exhibition first and the hospital second. The hospital tour exit is well away from both entrances, whereas you will still be close to them when you leave the Dunkirk exhibition. On busy days, a queuing system operates and you may have to sit around until it's your turn to go underground. Both tours are worth the wait. They're informative and inventive, employing technology and a fast pace to keep people entertained throughout.

After entering the tunnels where Operation Dynamo was planned and executed, you're played audio clips from the outbreak of World War II and are shown footage explaining how Britain and Germany arrived at a point of conflict in 1939. The sequence of events leading up to the Dunkirk evacuation is introduced and visitors get a real sense of how crucial the operation was. As you move along the network of tunnels, there are regular stops as sound effects and video projections on the chalk walls tell the evacuation story in a suitably dramatic style. Unveiled in 2011, this is a modern, hi-tech exhibition that does a remarkable job of educating visitors. Spitfires can be heard soaring overhead, the sound of anti-aircraft fire booms out and wartime footage shows scenes from the beaches of Dunkirk. You'll start to appreciate the cramped conditions within these narrow tunnels and the pressure of working here at such a difficult time. The tour moves on, passing rooms showing what the facilities were like during the days of Operation Dynamo. The experience would be remarkable enough if it were housed in a London museum, but learning about this key historical event in the actual rooms where it was planned has an added poignancy.

The hospital tunnels are brought to life by a story played as you make your way around operating theatres and wards for the sick. The tale follows the fortunes of a badly wounded soldier who has just arrived in the hospital from battle. Attempts are made to save his life in an echo of what must have been a common narrative in these former emergency rooms. This one may not be for the squeamish, though. There

Two underground WWII attractions included as part of the Dover Castle admission fee

The control room for Operation Dynamo, from where the evacuation of Dunkirk was overseen

A bunker tunnelled deep into the white cliffs used as a wartime hospital

opposite Dover Castle has been close to the action of many conflicts over the centuries.

is quite a lot of talk about blood, injuries and operations. You won't see anything that will put you off your ice cream afterwards, but the dark, confined environment may not be everybody's cup of tea.

The exit from the hospital tunnel is via steps, though there is also a lift for those who can't manage the stairs. Once you're out in the fresh air again, look for the statue of the man behind the rescue operation at Dunkirk, Vice Admiral Bertram Ramsey, who stands tall and proud, gazing towards Dunkirk. On a clear day from here, you can easily make out France on the horizon. This brings home just how close Dover's network of wartime tunnels was to the action in Europe as well as the pivotal role the tunnels played in shaping the war's outcome.

GOING DEEPER...

Following the outbreak of war with Germany on 1 September 1939, the British Expeditionary Force was sent to France and Belgium. Initially, though, nothing happened. A long eight months of waiting saw forces positioned along the border with Germany, but no major offensive was launched. It became known as the Phoney War. On 10 May 1940, however, part of the German army moved through the Netherlands and Belgium, drawing the Allies up to confront it. A second German force went through Luxembourg and entered France at Sedan, before driving north towards the coast. British Forces were surrounded and, as the Germans took Boulogne and Calais on 25 May, a desperate situation was created. The port of Dunkirk became the only point where the British soldiers could reach home.

The Royal Navy's operation to rescue the soldiers from Dunkirk was codenamed Operation Dynamo and the tunnel complex beneath Dover Castle was used as its headquarters. These tunnels inside the famous white cliffs had been dug to house soldiers during the Napoleonic Wars of the early 19th century, but they took on a whole new lease of life in 1940 when they housed the operation masterminding the rescue of hundreds of thousands of men from France. Vice Admiral Bertram Ramsey took charge of the operation and spent a week making plans to get ships across the English Channel. On 26 May, he was told to put his plan into action.

It was an incredibly difficult operation to carry out. The thousands of men waiting on the beach and in the town were vulnerable to German air attacks. The main docks had been crippled and so a breakwater had to be used instead. Soldiers needed ferrying to the larger ships that couldn't come in close to the shore, but famously assisting the operation were hundreds of smaller vessels, soon dubbed the Little Ships, and manned by volunteers that made their way across the sea to bring the stranded soldiers back to British shores.

The evacuation of Dunkirk took time to gain momentum and initial progress was slow. Only 8,000 men were rescued on the first day of the mission, but after that the operation started to gather pace. Between 26 May and 4 June, an astonishing 338,226 troops were brought home from France. Some 933 vessels were involved, many making several journeys under the control of incredibly brave volunteers. Sadly, 236 of them were lost – a reminder that many paid a high price during this remarkable wartime operation.

overleaf Tunnels were dug into the white cliffs of Dover during the Napoleonic wars and converted into state of the art control rooms during World War II.

below Secret tunnels were mined out of the iconic white cliffs of Dover.

THE LOWDOWN

LOCATION The tour must be booked online. The meeting point is beneath Brighton Pier

OPENING HOURS Tours on selected days between May and Sept

PRICE £12/£6
ADDRESS 260 Kings Road Arches, Brighton, BN2 1TD

TEL 01903 272124
EMAIL sewertours@southernwater.co.uk
WEBSITE www.southernwater.co.uk/brighton-sewer-tours

28

BRIGHTON SEWERS

AN OPPORTUNITY NOT TO BE FLUSHED AWAY

This underground tour of the Victorian Brighton sewer system is one of the most unusual journeys beneath Britain you're likely to take. If you're visiting Brighton for a limited amount of time, it's important to check the dates and times that these tours run. The treks into the sewers must be accompanied by expert guides and they are only available on certain dates between May and September. Because of their limited availability, the unique nature of the trip and the Victorian splendour of the sewers themselves, this is an extremely popular trip that regularly fills up. The numbers going underground are limited to 25 per tour, meaning that only around 1,800 people a year get to see what goes on beneath Brighton's streets. Plan your visit well in advance and book your underground tour online. Then hope it stays dry: some of the tours are cancelled for health and safety reasons after heavy rain because the subterranean tunnels are likely to flood.

After you've booked, you'll be told when and where to meet for your tour. As you may expect for a tour of a working sewer, there is no glamorous entrance or visitor centre. You

get together beneath Brighton Pier and go beyond a gate towards a door with a small sign above it, confirming you're in the right place. In the reception area, you'll be kitted out with not only hard hats but also gloves – a small reminder that the place you're about to enter does have health risks associated with it. There are rats living down there; you may see them, though they don't often pop out on the public tours. And, yes, expect some pongy smells – this is a sewer, after all. But after a while you'll find it's fairly well ventilated.

After some initial information about the building of the sewers and changes made over the years, you're shown a short video. It's not for the squeamish and it's not what you should watch after a heavy meal! The short film shows what happens to the fat, oil and grease that people put down their drains. The film follows this troublesome waste as it makes its way into the sewers and builds up into what can be a sizeable problem.

The group is then divided in two and you set off for an up-close view of where the city's human waste goes after flushing. You head to various overflows and sewage tunnels, picking up fascinating facts along the way about how the waste management system has cleaned up its act since the days when everything was simply dumped out to sea. Two things stand out as you develop your knowledge of these south coast sewers. The first is the complexity of the system devised by the Victorian engineers. No pumps were initially used in the sewers, which relied on gravity and the careful measurement of the tunnels, which needed to drop by three feet every mile. The other great wonder to look at is the manner in which these Victorian 'gun barrel sewers' were constructed. No tunnelling was done here. A trench was dug all the way along the route of the sewer by navvies drafted in

opposite The brick-built Victorian sewers beneath Brighton are still used and expected to function for hundreds of years to come.

below Tours set off beneath the iconic pier.

for the job. The brick sewage barrels were then built in an egg shape for extra strength, and covered over. Such a successful job was made of this sewage network that experts reckon it will function for 500 years from when it was built.

As you negotiate the labyrinth, reference will be made by the guide to what's above your head at street level, so if you're not from Brighton it may be worth familiarising yourself with the area around the pier, the roundabout and Steine Gardens ahead of taking the tour. You'll then be able to see where key things are happening underground, such as where important overflow areas are and where a large, lengthy sewage barrel from London meets the local Brighton network.

The majority of people living in Brighton will have no idea where these hidden channels run, even though this unusual attraction is widely known about locally. But this is not a tour that relies on visits from curious residents living nearby: it has an international appeal, attracting visitors from all four corners of the globe who wish to experience this important piece of British engineering history. Prepare a list of any questions you might have and quiz your tour guide, who will be a fount of sewage knowledge.

GOING DEEPER...

In the middle of the 19th century, human waste in Brighton was drained into cesspools at the back of people's houses. It was a problematic and unhealthy system that Victorian engineers wanted to bring to an end. In 1860, the town council decided to create a new sewage system that would drain waste into the sea. The resulting underground labyrinth of sewers was so well designed and built that it is still in use today and as effective as ever, although the treatment of the water is now far more thorough. Without power tools to make their job easier, the workers who tackled the ambitious Brighton sewer project relied solely on manual labour. If the tunnels were being constructed today, they would feature concrete segments connected by machinery. But the sewers you walk through on the tour are brick built and have a lot more character, with more human involvement in their construction than the waste systems built on modern housing estates.

Hundreds of tonnes of sand were taken from beaches along the coast to make the vast quantities of cement that

No pumps were initially used in the sewers, which relied on gravity and the careful measurement of the tunnels, which needed to drop by three feet every mile.

There's a definite whiff of waste on the tour, but this is a working sewer after all!

were needed, and if you look at the mortar between the bricks you will still be able to see sea shells sandwiched in there. Bricklayers working in the sewers were paid for each 12ft section they completed. Each of these lengths would see them rewarded with between ten and 15 shillings, the equivalent of 50–75p. The fastest bricklayers in the 1870s could expect to earn £4 and ten shillings a week, with general labourers earning around half this amount.

There are dangers in the sewers, but Southern Water has an alarm system in place to warn of any build-up of gases or any sudden rainfall that could lead to flooding. If there is heavy rain leading up to the tour, there is a chance that it will be cancelled for health and safety reasons. In that case, Southern Water will contact you by phone or email to rearrange your tour time. Higher levels of rainfall over autumn and winter mean that there are no tours arranged between October and April. These are working sewers – the tunnel between Hove and Portobello is an emergency relief valve in heavy rain – and this is why you may come across a rat or two during your tour. Don't let this put you off as it's not a regular occurrence. The route of the tour is washed down before each tour takes place and this usually scares off the rodents that many people are afraid of.

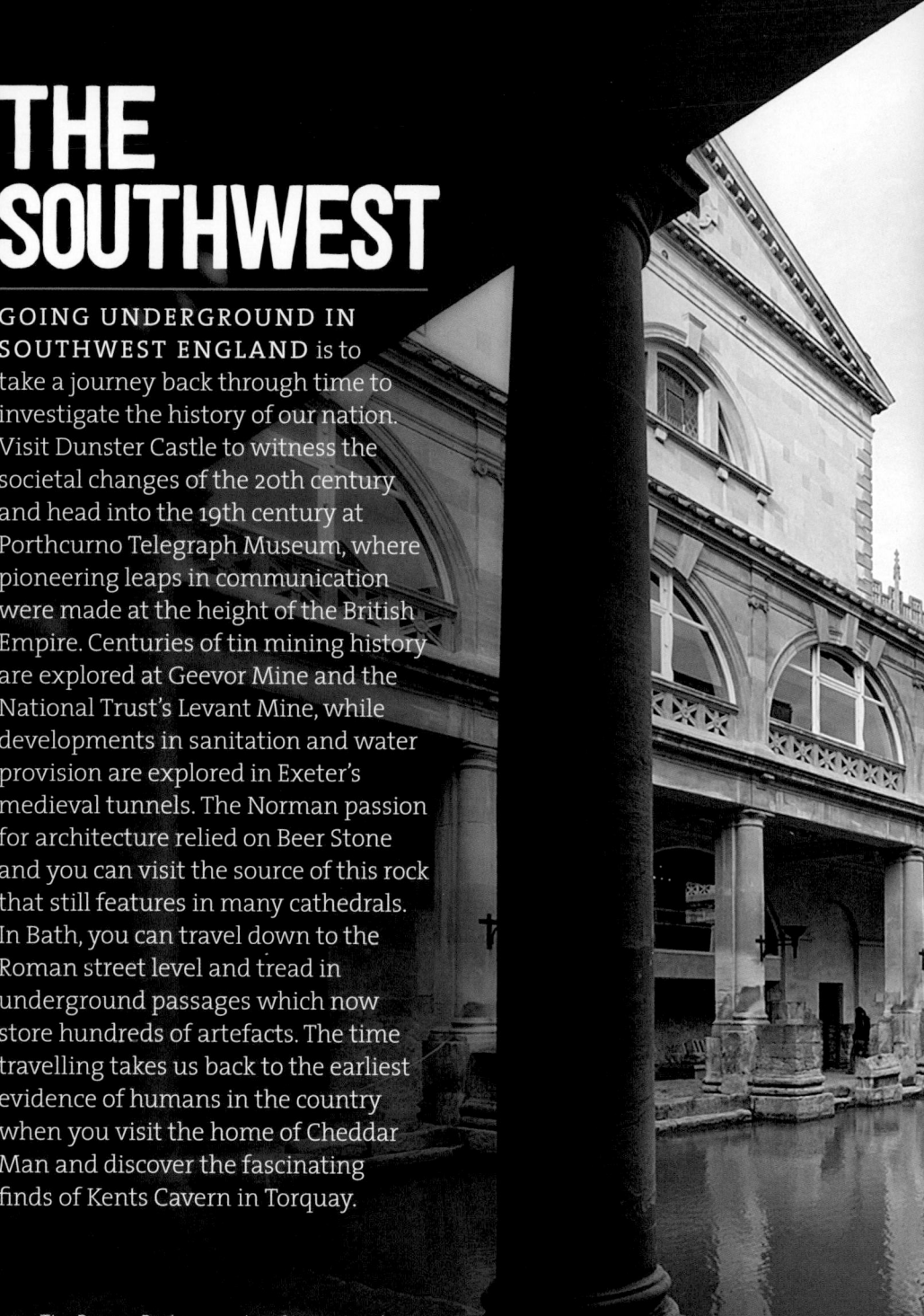

THE SOUTHWEST

GOING UNDERGROUND IN SOUTHWEST ENGLAND is to take a journey back through time to investigate the history of our nation. Visit Dunster Castle to witness the societal changes of the 20th century and head into the 19th century at Porthcurno Telegraph Museum, where pioneering leaps in communication were made at the height of the British Empire. Centuries of tin mining history are explored at Geevor Mine and the National Trust's Levant Mine, while developments in sanitation and water provision are explored in Exeter's medieval tunnels. The Norman passion for architecture relied on Beer Stone and you can visit the source of this rock that still features in many cathedrals. In Bath, you can travel down to the Roman street level and tread in underground passages which now store hundreds of artefacts. The time travelling takes us back to the earliest evidence of humans in the country when you visit the home of Cheddar Man and discover the fascinating finds of Kents Cavern in Torquay.

right The Roman Baths are a key feature on the city of Bath's skyline, but more can be learned about the Romans by heading beneath the surface of the streets.

THE LOWDOWN

LOCATION In the centre of the city of Bath

OPENING HOURS Mar–Oct 9–5; Nov–Feb 9.30–5; summer holiday opening until 9; underground tours on Weds (included in price) but must be booked in advance

PRICE £16.50/£14.50 /£10.25, family £48
ADDRESS Abbey Church-yard, Bath, BA1 1LZ
TEL 01225 477785

EMAIL roman baths_bookings @bathnes.gov.uk
WEBSITE www. romanbaths.co.uk

29

ROMAN BATHS ABOVE AND BELOW TOURS

ALL ROADS LEAD TO BATH

The City of Bath is a World Heritage Site – not just the Roman Baths complex, which is the focus of this underground venture, but the whole city centre. The historical significance of the Roman ruins and the Georgian architecture throughout the city centre earned Bath the prestigious UNESCO status in 1987. It's a charming city to walk around, with pictur-esque photographic opportunities at nearly every corner. When constructing this delightful city in the 18th century, Georgian architects built exquisite homes above the level developed by the Romans. The result is a rich historical cache of ruins and artefacts beneath today's street level.

Before making your visit to the city, it's worth contacting the Roman Baths in advance to check what tours are available. There are a range of different themed guided tours offering access to behind-the-scenes areas and tunnels beneath the city that are not available to visitors with standard tickets. The

Above and Below Tour delivers exactly what it promises. First it takes you out of the Roman Baths complex to show you where an ancient temple once stood and what can be found close by the site in the 21st century – in this case, Primark. You then head back into the museum and sneak through a side door most people will not have noticed. This takes you into a network of passageways that are at the same level as the Roman pavements built when the settlement was called Aquae Sulis. Centuries later, the Georgians built over them, turning these one-time Roman walkways into tunnels beneath grand structures.

Much of these off-limits areas are functional now, rather than pretty and well-presented. There's a water-treatment machine making the city's famous mineral water fit for consumption. Pipes and wires are tucked away down here to allow the modern-day functions of a major tourist attraction to be carried out seamlessly. And a whole section of this underground space is dedicated to storing hundreds of incomplete stone statues, buildings and monuments. Some of these

The best preserved ancient baths and temple complex in northern Europe

Artefacts found beneath the city streets give an insight into Roman life

The hidden underground section can be visited on specially booked tours

opposite The warm spring water from beneath the hills of Bath has a green appearance because of the many minerals it contains.

below Visitors can also gaze upon the steam rooms where Romans relaxed.

are Roman, some are Anglo-Saxon and others hail from the Victorian era. All are labelled and tagged meticulously. Some of the passageway you are walking along has been cemented over, but in places you can see the original Roman stones that people walked on 2,000 years ago.

With a hard hat being essential to guard against contact with the low ceiling, this tour is not for the faint-hearted. It's very warm down there, and in places it can smell damp and musty. Worse news for many is that you may come across the occasional rat or two. These are warnings given out by the tour guide at the start of the one-hour pre-booked event and those who did not want to come across a rodent are given the opportunity to stay outside the passageways. Because of the rats, you'll be urged not to touch anything in certain areas and to wash your hands straight after the tour. The Above and Below Tours don't take place every day, and in the summer months they tend to happen towards the end of the day. This would be an ideal time to book one of these tours as it avoids the crowds in the early afternoon and gives you the chance to see the main Roman bath illuminated by torchlight.

below The Romans created an intricate bath house system, much of it still in place.

Even if you are not able to book onto the underground tour you can still savour the delights of the Roman ruins found beneath Bath's streets. One of the actual Roman walkways – now four metres below today's street level – has been excavated and is on the self-guided audio tour open to all visitors. You can look at the steps, pathways, drains and even a sacrificial table, imagining Romans going about their daily business on this very spot underneath the hustle and bustle of the modern city of Bath.

GOING DEEPER...

The water you can see in the Roman Baths appears to be green in colour, but it is actually colourless when it emerges from the ground. The green tint is acquired through the growth of algae caused by daylight and the heat of the water. Visitors were allowed to bathe in the water until the 1970s, but now you're not even allowed to dip your fingers in because of strict health and safety regulations. If you would like to sample the water in its pure state, you'll get a chance to fill a cup of the mineral-rich liquid at the end of the museum experience, or you could also head to the Pump Room.

above The source of hot water is the reason why the Romans developed the city and built the bath house.

The spa water that has given Bath its reputation flows at 13 litres per second, meaning that well over one million litres emerges daily. And it's hot, too! This is the only hot spring in the country, so it's no wonder the Romans were tempted to build a major site here. At its source, the temperature of the spring water has been measured at 46°C. If you're visiting the baths on a chilly day, you will see plenty of steam rising from the water into the city air as you walk around the edge.

There are 43 minerals in the water, which is why it developed a reputation as having health benefits. High amounts of calcium, sulphate, sodium and chloride are present. The water does not have high levels of dissolved metals, with the exception of iron, that gives the orange staining you'll see in several places around the site. Many people looking at the King's Bath see the green water bubbling away and presume that it's boiling in there. But the water is not that hot. Instead, the bubbles are caused by gases escaping.

When the Romans built their bath house here, it would have taken a huge logistical effort. Plenty of local timber would have been used from nearby woodland, but other materials would have been more difficult to obtain. Building stone was transported from the hills to the south of the Avon, clay tiles used were fetched from Wiltshire and lead was brought in from the Mendips. Surveyors, plumbers and many other types of tradesmen were involved in the ambitious development, which was part of a wave of construction initiatives intended to demonstrate how committed the Romans were to boosting their new north European province. The monumental building programme came together successfully and was completed by AD 75, when the Romans used the water of the hot springs to relax in and treat their ailments for the first time.

below The underground tour takes you to places not seen by most visitors.

| LOCATION | OPENING HOURS | PRICE | ADDRESS Cheddar, BS27 3QF | THE LOWDOWN |
| On the B3135 heading east out of Cheddar | Daily 10–5 | £19.95/£14.95, online discount available | TEL 01934 742343 EMAIL info@cheddargorge.co.uk WEBSITE www.cheddargorge.co.uk | |

30

CHEDDAR GORGE AND CAVES

UP CLOSE WITH CHEDDAR MAN

You cannot fail to be impressed by Cheddar Gorge. Whether you descend into it from the Mendip Hills or gaze up towards the rocky sides from the village of Cheddar, the views are jaw-dropping. It's the largest gorge in the UK and it was formed by meltwater floods following glacial periods over the last million years. As well as shaping the landscape you can see above ground, water has also carved a formidable treasure deep within these limestone hills.

The Cheddar Gorge and Caves ticket includes access to several attractions that help you to explore this landscape, its formation and the people and animals that have lived here over the years. Top of the list is Gough's Cave. It's the biggest and most fascinating of the underground features in Cheddar Gorge. The impressive cave network is named after Richard Cox Gough, the local explorer who found the entrance, exca- vated his way into it over a number of years and eventually opened it up to the public.

Today's visitors are in for a totally different experience to that of those early tourists as the latest technology is employed

A self-guided audio tour tells the story of how the enchanting features in Gough's Cave were discovered

Lights, lasers and films transform Cox's Cave to tell the story of hunting humans

Ticket includes several attractions, including a museum about early humans living in the area

to create a state-of-the-art visitor attraction in these natural surroundings. On entering Gough's Cave, visitors pick up an audio guide and take a self-guided tour around the cave network, keying in the appropriate number displayed at various locations. There's no shortage of tales to listen to from the audio guide, and they are split into short talks for the adults and children in the group. The signs featuring audio-guide numbers also have a brief description of what's in the recording, so you can pick and choose if you wish. Most of the audio guide is spoken in a light-hearted manner through the eyes of Richard Gough, in a strong Somerset accent. It makes good listening as he describes the struggle to excavate the cave and the reward of his discovery.

The two chambers at the end of Gough's Cave are the features to get most excited about, although the stalagmites you pass on the way are well worth taking time over. The first of these chambers is cathedral-like in size. The domed roof towering above prompted Gough to name it after St Paul's Cathedral. Right at the end of the passage, just before you turn around to retrace your steps, is the Diamond Chamber. You won't find diamonds in there, but you will be amazed by the calcite flowstone formations that appear to cascade down the far wall.

Further down the hill at Cheddar Gorge, Cox's Cave was once the premier attraction in the days before Gough's Cave was discovered. Today, there's a risk that the relatively small Cox's Cave could be an anti-climax after a visit to Gough's Cave. To overcome this, the owners have transformed Cox's Cave into the 'Dreamhunters' experience. Around every corner on your way through the cave, a fresh audio-visual presentation is given to describe the lives of our ancestors and how they hunted animals locally to survive. Their encounters with bears, horses, woolly mammoths and wolves are brought to life with care and respect. The sometimes brutal nature of their existence is explained crisply and clearly. All this takes place against a backdrop of incredible cave formations that are decorated with animal skins and lit in dramatic colours.

It may be a struggle to complete all the attractions at Cheddar Gorge in just one day. However, your ticket, which allows you to do everything that is on offer once, lasts for a

previous page A climb to the top of the gorge is a must during your visit.

generous ten years, so you've got plenty of time to try and fit everything in. If you're just passing through and haven't got the gift of time on your side, the Museum of Prehistory – on the opposite side of the road to the caves – is worth prioritising. In there, you'll learn about the world-famous Cheddar Man, whose remains were discovered in Gough's Cave, and about the animals that have lived in the caves through the ages. Look out for the cave bear skeleton that surprises people as it hides behind a corner halfway through the exhibits!

GOING DEEPER...

Of all the finds in the caves at the gorge, Cheddar Man is the most famous and significant. He was discovered in 1903, a short distance into Gough's Cave on the left-hand side. A model of the skeleton that was unearthed is on show to give an idea of the position. Tests on the bones have dated Cheddar Man to the Mesolithic – over 7,000 years bc. Recent DNA research has also found that Cheddar Man does have distant relations living today in the Cheddar area. Appropriately, a history teacher has been identified as a descendant of this most famous of Cheddar ancestors. The tests were conducted in 1996 and focused on DNA taken from one of Cheddar Man's molars. Another tooth

below A truly significant find, Cheddar Man is the oldest complete skeleton found in the UK.

found in the cave, which dating techniques showed to be some 3,000 years older than Cheddar Man's, was also studied. Cheddar Man's was not the oldest bone material found here, but the discovery was crucially important because Cheddar Man's skeleton was complete and in such good condition.

From detailed examination of the skeleton, it appears that Cheddar Man may have suffered a violent death. A hole in his skull suggests his end may not have been natural. He was also suffering from an infection at the time. Displays in the local museum point to evidence of cannibalism in the area during the time in which Cheddar Man was living. Other human remains have evidence of bite marks. Exactly what happened to Cheddar Man in his final hours may never be known for certain, but as Britain's oldest complete human skeleton, his place in history is guaranteed.

A full-size replica of Cheddar Man as he would have looked when he was alive, together with the weapons and tools he would have had to hand, is on display at the museum across the road from the cave where he was discovered. It greets you as you walk in and it is a startling sight. Even a casual glance around the museum informs visitors that life would not have been easy for Cheddar Man. There was a lot to contend with in terms of predators and climatic conditions, making survival challenging. To see the real skeleton of Cheddar Man, you'll have to leave Somerset's Mendip Hills and head for London, for the actual remains are on display at the Natural History Museum in Kensington. Visitors there can see Cheddar Man standing in the gallery about human evolution, a fitting resting place for one of the country's most significant historical residents.

above Cheddar cheese is left to mature in the moist cave atmosphere.

opposite Lakes below the famous gorge throw up kaleidoscopic reflections.

WOOKEY HOLE

18

THE LAIR OF SCARY WITCHES AND TASTY CHEESE

The astonishing cave network at Wookey Hole is a well-established attraction providing a great family day out in the Mendips, but is just one in a long list of activities offered to visitors. The ticket to Wookey Hole enables you to go on a 40-minute guided tour underground to kick off your day, followed by a series of smaller attractions such as a paper-making counter, mini-golf, a soft play area, a 4D cinema experience and a mock-seaside zone complete with penny amusements and a hall of mirrors. It's the stuff of dreams for a family with young children on a wet day of their holiday.

After entering the Wookey Hole attraction, you're directed up the hill to the cave entrance. Expect a small wait here at busy times and be prepared to encounter a pirate wanting to take a family photo. The size of your tour group can be large in the school holidays – it's common for over 60 people to be shown around at a time, so it's a good idea to get near the front, where it's easier to listen. When it's time to enter the cave, the first thing you come face to face with is the model of the

THE LOWDOWN

LOCATION To the north-west of Wells, off the A371

OPENING HOURS Apr–Oct 10–5; Nov–Mar 10–4; weekends and school holidays from Dec until Feb half term

PRICE £19/£17/£15 **ADDRESS** Wookey Hole Caves, Wookey Hole, Wells, Somerset, BA5 1BB

TEL 01749 672243 **EMAIL** witch@wookey.co.uk **WEBSITE** www.wookey.co.uk

witch who was said to have made a home here. The legend of the witch is something the tour guide plays on for spooky effect, setting up the story and rounding it off with visions of flowstone and stalagmites that have formed into the shape of a witch's head and dog.

Various chambers are on show to the public, and all feature atmospheric lighting – whites, blues and reds – that offer a fresh approach around every corner. Some of the chambers are astonishingly immense, rising high above your head and revealing swirling hollows created by water forcefully eroding downwards. Others are more claustrophobic, with a low ceiling and a cylindrical shape. All are the result of water erosion processes, and this and other areas of the cave network are still prone to flooding, though it is thankfully a rare event. The last major flood was in the 1960s, when water levels rose to fill the caverns in just 20 minutes, so the guides giving tours today are trained to monitor a key rock in the cavern's pool to check that water levels are not worryingly close to covering it.

In the days when the caves were owned by Madame Tussauds, public tours used to finish a lot earlier than they do today, and followed the same route back to the entrance. However, frustrated by the lack of access to chambers further in, in 1974 the company decided to blast through the rock and open up more underground sites. As a result, on your way to the new exit you will pass over bridges in the middle of chambers that reveal blue-green pools below and a stalactite-dotted roof above. There is also an extraordinary feature of eroded limestone that was carved out during the Ice Age and that is thought to be the only one of its kind in the world found underground. Those wanting to have more of a caving trip than the traditional guided tour offers can pay to take part in a three-hour experience during which they wear professional equipment, tackle tough crawls and embark on tricky climbs.

The largest system of caves in the UK, explored extensively by divers over the decades

Cave conditions are ideal for ageing the local Cheddar cheese, which you can buy in the shop

A dizzying array of additional attractions, including museums and play areas

opposite Supernatural stories abound on this underground adventure.

below Intriguing formations lie in wait beneath Somerset's hills.

31 WOOKEY HOLE

Cave-aged Cheddar cheese is a local delicacy and available in the shop here and elsewhere. There's a whole passageway in the cave dedicated to this process, with shelf upon shelf of cheese lined up, dated and monitored. The team from the BBC children's TV programme *Blue Peter* came here to investigate the cheese-making process, but that is not the only programme to feature the underground landscape at Wookey Hole. When Tom Baker played the titular Timelord in *Doctor Who*, an episode was filmed in these rocky passageways and chambers beneath the Mendip hills. His dreaded enemy in the Wookey Hole caves was none other than the Cybermen. Hopefully there won't be any of them lingering around on your visit.

The exit from the cave network is further down the hill, and from there you walk into a valley occupied by a plethora of dinosaur models. The rest of your time at Wookey Hole can be spent on the wide range of other attractions. These include a small museum about cave diving and displays about the geological processes forming the caves and the Mendip Hills.

GOING DEEPER...

Because of the high water level within the cave system, many of the chambers in the network cannot be explored without diving equipment. Some of these elusive underwater chambers have been bypassed with the help of explosives, allowing visitors to reach more accessible chambers further along the lengthy system. We owe our knowledge of the caves at Wookey Hole to a number of keen divers who have fearlessly explored the waters. The first expedition set out in 1935 under the leadership of Graham Balcombe. At Wookey Hole, he made the first cave dive in the British Isles, using state-of-the-art breathing

below The tour of the cave system will take your breath away, while photo opportunities are plentiful.

apparatus developed by Siebe Gorman. It was a long way from modern-day diving equipment: a large brass helmet over his head had air delivered to it via a long tube. The suit he wore was made from rubber and canvas, his boots had lead weights to keep him anchored below the water and he frequently needed help to free his air supply from obstructions.

The early dives allowed the team to reach Chamber 7. Visitors to Wookey Hole today can look down from a high catwalk within the chamber and see down to the rock beneath the water, where that early expedition had to end. But there was still work to be done, and in 1948 Balcombe returned to the caves, this time using diving equipment that had been developed during the war. On this occasion the team managed to reach Chamber 9, an enormous space that is 100ft high with water 70ft deep. Discovering this chamber allowed cavers to form a base there from which to launch further diving expeditions, making the job much easier.

Exploration continues to this day, with cavers by now having found a series of 25 chambers. Beyond this, the system descends steeply into a dark abyss. A diving attempt in 2004 reached a depth of 249ft, but no diver has yet reached the bottom and found what lies beyond. The exploration of the caves at Wookey Hole is exciting and has yet to be concluded, but it is not without its costs. Divers have to contend with the limitations of going down so the deep, needing to make vital stops for decompression. A young diver on an expedition in 1981 sadly drowned making the attempt. He was the second diver to lose his life in this cave system, which still drives curious explorers on to discover what secrets it has to reveal.

above A cracker of an idea – Cheddar cheese now matures in the caves at Wookey Hole.

overleaf Serenely beautiful underground sights are mixed with spooky, supernatural stories on the Wookey Hole tour. This pool with a small, solitary boat is one of the first photo stops beneath the Somerset hills.

DUNSTER CASTLE RESERVOIR

23

SUBTERRANEAN VICTORIAN INGENUITY

With Victorian technology developing quickly to include such luxuries as bathrooms and taps, the owners of Dunster Castle needed a new method to bring water to their home. The result was typically elaborate.

A pipe over two miles long was built between the castle and a farm at the same height across the valley, allowing water to be transferred over to Dunster. The water was then deposited and stored in a new underground reservoir built in a mound close to the castle. With the prized H2O of the reservoir being at a higher elevation than all the taps in the castle, water pressure was not an issue and the problem of supply to this stronghold was solved. It was a relatively small-scale engineering feat compared with other grand achievements in the Victorian era, but the underground reservoir at Dunster Castle was nonetheless a remarkable success. It's also a relatively new subterranean attraction. Visitors have only been able to see the underwater reservoir since 2016, when it was opened to mark the 40th anniversary of the National Trust owning Dunster Castle.

THE LOWDOWN

LOCATION
On the A396 just south of Minehead

OPENING HOURS Apr–Oct 10–5; between Nov and early Mar the castle is only accessible on a timed tour and grounds close at dusk

PRICE £12.80/£6.40/£31.90 National Trust members free

ADDRESS Dunster Castle, Dunster, Minehead, TA24 6SL

TEL 01643 823314

EMAIL enquiries@nationaltrust.org.uk

WEBSITE www.nationaltrust.org.uk/dunster-castle

Victorian reservoir constructed underground in a hill above the famous castle

Provided water to the house in the 19th century and opened to the public in 2016

Part of a very popular National Trust property with guided tours of house, as well as gardens and a café

There are many steep gradients at Dunster Castle. The watermill building and the café by the river are located pretty much at sea level, while the castle and gardens tower above them up the hill. Getting to the different features at the castle can be a challenge, but walking around the landscaped grounds is a great deal of fun. You get to the reservoir either by a circular, winding walkway or via a more direct set of steep steps. The spiralling walkway to the underground reservoir leaves the front of the castle and arcs round beyond a pet cemetery before ending up at a door in the hillside. As you go in, you can tell instantly that the National Trust has taken great care in preserving this unusual space. A metal walkway takes you down into the now dry reservoir, below the line of the original high watermark. At the bottom, you'll stand on a metal platform, where swirling blue lights are projected onto the floor beneath your feet to give the illusion of water rippling. The walls were covered with clay to make the reservoir more likely to retain the water, but this material gave some Victorian visitors the opportunity to etch their name and the date onto it. More tragic marks on the wall are the desperate scratches of a badger which got stuck in here and sadly died.

opposite Getting water to Dunster Castle proved a challenging conundrum.

left Investment allowed modern-day visitors inside the reservoir for the first time.

You're invited to press a button that will start a short audio presentation about the origins of the reservoir. It's informative and gives a good account of why the reservoir is here. The investment by the National Trust to make this one of the attractions at Dunster Castle has paid off. Opening this up to the public, complete with lighting and spoken information, does bring a quirky additional dimension to a visit to Dunster Castle.

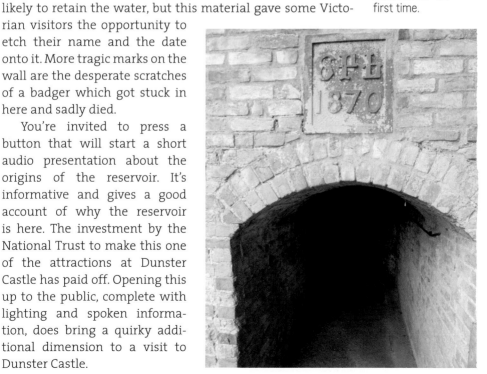

As you guide yourself around the house and see some of the Victorian living conditions, the need for a thoroughly reliable water supply becomes apparent. The kitchen staff were expected to cook for parties of up to 100 people and water was important for these events to be a success. The story of Dunster Castle being fitted out with the latest modern appliances is also told. Toilets, taps and a bath were all luxuries installed in the castle and, of course, all needed large amounts of water. The reservoir allowed the family to stay in their hilltop home while having access to the modern facilities that were making their way into large houses elsewhere in the country.

GOING DEEPER...

The reservoir sits around four metres below the surface of the garden, where people are walking above your head. Originally, this mound was the site of the motte and bailey castle, which dates back to Norman times. If engineers wanted to build the reservoir in the 21st century there is no way they would get permission – the Norman site of the castle is now a scheduled monument, restricting what can be done here. There were no such restrictions in Victorian days, of course, and the emphasis was very much on technological achievement.

When full, this underground reservoir was capable of holding 40,000 gallons of water – or over 180,000 litres. With all that liquid in the structure, the waterline would have come above the heads of today's visitors. The door leading into the reservoir has the inscription '1870' above it, referring to when the innovative development was completed. This fits in with other advances made by the then owner George Fownes Luttrell in the 1860s and 1870s. At the time, Dunster Castle was enjoying great prosperity and Luttrell wanted to take advantage of Victorian developments in technology. An architect was employed to modernise parts of the castle, bringing the kitchens and bathrooms up to the highest standards of the day. But a reliable and plentiful source of water was needed to allow these updated rooms to function properly. It's easy to see why attention turned to the building of this reservoir.

The reservoir was not just for the castle's benefit, though. By 1897 it was supplying the local water company, and homes in Minehead were getting running water as a result. The water going into Dunster's reservoir came from a farm two miles

> When full, this under-ground reservoir was capable of holding 40,000 gallons of water – or over 180,000 litres.

away on the other side of the valley. A pipe was laid all the way along the valley floor, and the water readily flowed into the reservoir because the farm was the same height above sea level as the castle. The original pipework was made from cast iron and is thought to have suffered from a series of leaks, so replacements had to be built. The later pipes were made from asbestos cement, and remains of both types can be seen coming into the reservoir.

The reservoir was sold off to the Somerset Water Board in 1967, but by 1976 it had been abandoned. Visitors were not allowed into this space until 2016, following an investment of £25,000 by the National Trust to open it up once more.

BEER QUARRY CAVES

THE DETAIL IS IN THE STONE

Up a quiet, narrow country lane leading out of the lovely village of Beer, the car park at Beer Quarry Caves is pleasantly humble. There are no big, bold statements on posters, no plastic dinosaurs vying for your attention, no vending machines selling things you don't need. There are only two portable toilets and a sign advising you to make use of them because there aren't any at the main building. The tour doesn't stop at any, either. This is a down-to-earth place, with more than a few surprising secrets below the surface.

A small shop and café provide just enough diversion to pass the time before the tour departs. Hard hats are given out and the group walks down a slope and round the corner to get down to the quarry and caves. As you approach the large fenced-off entrance, the temperature difference on a sunny day is striking. The chill can be felt well before heading inside, and it continues throughout the tour.

After an hour of being in the damp underground caves, you'll emerge once more into what seems like a comparatively tropical south Devon climate.

THE LOWDOWN

LOCATION Between Sidmouth and Lyme Regis on the A3052; the caves are signed from the main road

OPENING HOURS Apr–Oct 10–3.30 (4.30 in school holidays), out of season tours by prior arrangement

PRICE £8/£6, family £25.20

ADDRESS Quarry Lane, Beer, Seaton, Devon, EX12 3AT

TEL 01297 680282

EMAIL info@beer quarrycaves.co.uk

WEBSITE www.beer quarrycaves.co.uk

The first part of the tour – just inside the entrance – houses a small museum. Examples of Beer stone are placed all around, with explanations of how good the local rock is for carving. Photographs on the wall show where the famous local stone has been used around the world. The really eye-catching exhibit in this small underground collection, though, is the huge section of a medieval ornamental arch, carved from Beer stone and formerly part of a nearby church.

The home of Beer stone, quarried and used in buildings since Roman times

Two dozen cathedrals in the UK have Beer stone in their construction

When cut, it is easy to sculpt the rock, which then dries out and hardens

The guide leads the group through the caves, and each zone in the labyrinth is where a different era of quarrymen took out the rock. Initially you're in the halls cut by Romans, identified by the large arched doorways typical of their style. The more rugged look of the Anglo-Saxons follows before you reach the time when Normans cut huge amounts of rock away for the construction of cathedrals.

Although no stone is currently cut from Beer, the tour does reach a more modern section of the caves, where saws became the tool of choice and replaced the more cumbersome pickaxe. Graffiti on the wall creates a link with those who worked down

opposite Different eras of quarrying are easy to spot in the cave.

left Metal bars instead of a door allow bats to fly in and out.

here in what would have been noisy conditions plagued with the thick smoke from lamps.

Seemingly every turn has a story connected to it, and not all are associated with quarrying. During times of religious persecution, Catholics used part of the caves as a safe haven and place of worship. A less godly use of the premises was employed by infamous local smuggler Jack Rattenbury when he utilised the vast expanse of underground tunnels to hide away contraband goods. It's virtually an underground maze, and woe betide anybody who loses their way in here without a decent source of light. On the wall in some places you'll see some quite alarming arrows pointing the way out in case such an emergency arises. Make sure you stick with your group! The lighting on the tour comes from single bulbs hanging from wires in a plain, atmospheric display. Huge piles of waste rock have filled up and blocked off additional tunnels, sealing off yet more historical stories that may never be discovered.

If you're interested in wildlife, it may be worth ringing ahead to find out if it's the bat season, for at certain times of the year, the caves are home to a number of different bat species and bat tours are put on that give an insight into these fascinating animals. Greater horseshoe and lesser horseshoe bats are the main species, but the Natterer's bat and the whiskered bat are among the others to have been spotted in the cave.

below Following the twists and turns of this true labyrinth, summer visitors will find the quarry a chilly place.

left Facilities are limited in the quarry, giving it a very authentic feel and avoiding the trappings of tourism.

When they're in residence, dozens of bats occupy the cave and make themselves at home along the wires between light bulbs. Counts have put the number of bats living in the cave at over 300. If you arrive in the middle of summer when the bats are elsewhere, you'll have to make do with a picture on the wall of the cave that shows what it's like when the webbed winged mammals are here. But if you arrive at the beginning or end of the tourist season, you may well see one or more of them flying around. The bats can, of course, get out of the cave to source food as the entrance is closed off by railings rather than a solid wall. And don't worry about them bothering you, as they tend to keep themselves away from visiting groups.

The tour of Beer Quarry Caves is packed with historical facts that are both relevant and interesting, highlighting the role this small community has played in important events throughout the ages. The guides speak of possible future funding applications that could transform Beer Quarry Caves by developing the visitor facilities. For although this is currently a small visitor attraction, it has the potential to share its underground wonders with many more tourists.

GOING DEEPER...

Beer stone has an outstanding reputation amongst stonemasons around the world because of the way it can be carved with fine detail and used in the most ornate of buildings. The rock itself, a light-coloured, fine-textured limestone, dates back to the Cretaceous Period when dinosaurs roamed the earth. Early layers are thought to be 120 million years old. The seam that runs north to south through Beer is between four and six metres

> It's virtually an underground maze, and woe betide anybody who loses their way in here without a decent source of light.

thick, and because it is saturated it has been an extremely useful asset for stonemasons down the years. When it is quarried, Beer stone is relatively soft and an ideal material for those wanting to carve intricate designs into it. The key quality of Beer stone is the way it reacts to the air once it's taken away from the cave environment. After it's been carved, it dries a lovely white colour and hardens quickly, making it up to five times stronger than it is when it is first cut.

Used far and wide, Beer stone has become particularly well known for its use in cathedrals. Because it can be carved finely, the stone is ideally suited to these buildings that require stonemasons to craft ornate arches, intricate patterns and detailed statues. Of the 44 cathedrals in Britain, Beer stone can be found in no less than 24 of them. Westminster Abbey and St Paul's Cathedral are two high-profile buildings making use of Beer stone. Other cathedrals around the country that incorporate Beer stone in some form include those at Norwich and Winchester. But it's the nearby cathedral at Exeter that utilised it most extensively. Standing in front of Exeter Cathedral, it's impossible not to be impressed by the array of statues made from Beer stone that adorn the front of the building. The high cost of transporting heavy Beer stone has limited its use in the nation's smaller building projects, but a number of developments in the local area relied on it for decora-

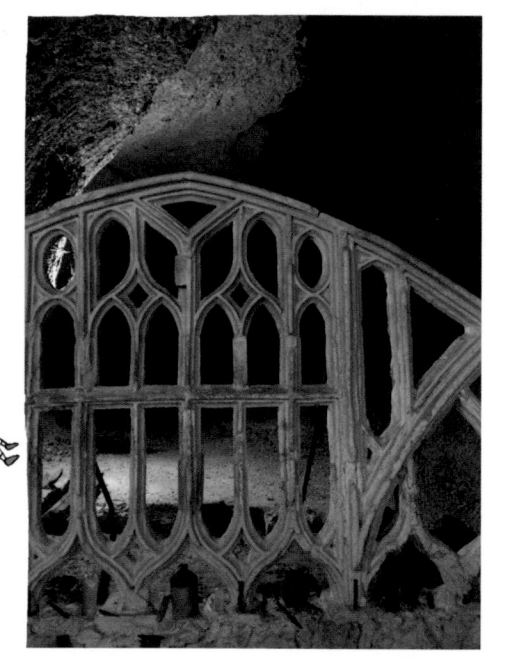

above The detail in medieval stonework is astonishing – intricately carved Beer stone features in many cathedrals.

tive work. The Guildhall at Exeter and Beer's Bovey House are two secular examples, while smaller churches to have called upon Beer stone include St Michael's in Beer and St Mary's at Ottery St Mary. Further afield, Beer stone was used to carve the altarpiece for Christ Church Cathedral in St Louis, Missouri. The £75,000 project was funded by a woman who saw a carving in St Albans Cathedral and wanted to commission something similar for her place of worship in St Louis. The work was overseen by a Yorkshire sculpture, Harry Hems, who had developed a solid reputation for cathedral restoration. The reredos was worked on by stonemasons in Exeter between 1909 and 1911 before being carefully shipped out to the United States.

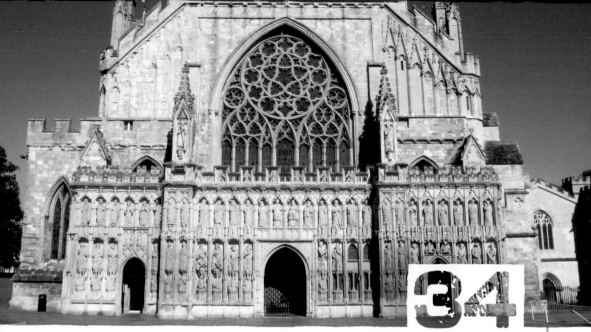

34

EXETER'S UNDERGROUND PASSAGES

EXPLORING EXETER'S MEDIEVAL WATERWAYS

Before it's your time to go to the Underground Passages building where the tours begin, it's a good idea to have a brief stroll around the area immediately around it in the centre of Exeter. Locate shops such as Hotel Chocolat, Waterstones and John Lewis as you familiarise yourself with the layout. These are some of the stores you'll be walking beneath on your tour, and it's worth finding them so that you have an idea of your location when the guide refers to them underground. As modern life carries on at the surface on the streets and in the shops, it's very hard to imagine the network of passages that twist and turn around four metres below your feet. But down beneath the grey streets and modern shopping centres are medieval passages that are the only example of their kind in Britain. As such, they are protected and attract a great deal of attention from tourists in the Southwest and beyond.

above The passages can be a tight squeeze but it's well worth making the journey into the past.

previous page The entrance to Exeter Cathedral is stunning and features stone from Beer Quarry.

When you're walking along the underground network there's not much room at all and you can see why visitor numbers on these tours are strictly capped. You'll have to walk in single file, and the taller people in the group will no doubt be glad of their hard hat at times. So tight are the passages at some points that not everybody will be able to see the tour guide. It will be a case of all squeezing in together so that you can listen to the guide's stories about the history of these compelling spaces beneath the city of Exeter. Expect a handful of other people to join you on this adventure beneath Britain, and make sure you book in advance – especially during school holidays, when the diary can fill up very quickly.

Arrive a few minutes before the start of your guided tour slot so you can be signed in. You then head down a few flights of stairs to a small museum about the passages' construction and the centuries-old methods of transporting water. A short film gives you a brief history of Exeter's Underground Passages and their significance to the development of the city. Then it's time to grab your hard hat and see them for yourself.

Water is at the heart of all these historical passages. Although you will not see any of the piping that carried the water from a natural spring to locations in the city, this is the exact route the pipes took. Originally, they were destined solely for the cathedral. Later, public drinking fountains benefited too from the clean source of water. If you had enough money you could even pay to have a branch of piping diverted to your house. Through all these times, when sanitation was poor and water-borne diseases killed scores, clean water was sought by all.

Passages built in the 14th and 15th centuries

Designed to bring clean water in from springs outside the city

The lead pipes carrying water could be easily accessed and repaired if leaking

The pipes underneath Exeter aided the population in medieval days and were used right through to the Victorian era. Although the pipes carrying the water were made from lead, which would not be allowed today, people at the time were far more likely to die from water-borne diseases than from lead poisoning. The cleanliness of the local water was such an issue for people in Victorian times that many chose to drink the local cider rather than water which may have been contaminated.

Towards the end of the tour, there's a challenge for the more nimble members of the group. If you're up to it, a diversion leads to a very low section of passageway which you can negotiate on your hands and knees. Don't worry if this isn't for you – there's an alternative route that involves much less crouching.

The experience lasts about 50 minutes in total. Then it's hard hats off so that the next group can use them, and you get to spend more time looking at the information on display in the museum. When you return to the surface, it's interesting to see where you have walked by finding the shops and street names that were mentioned. But above all, make sure you walk up the main street towards the cathedral. As well as appreciating the magnificence of this building, which is worth a visit in its own right, it gives you a sense of perspective about how far the passages carrying water actually stretched. In medieval times, with limited resources and expertise, this subterranean water network was quite an achievement.

below Intricately carved from Beer stone, these statues have looked upon Exeter for centuries.

GOING DEEPER...

The popularity of Exeter Cathedral for worshippers was increasing in the 12th century, with the result that the water supply became a big issue. Ever since Roman times, the folk of Exeter had used fresh water springs at St Sidwell's in the northeast of the city, and this was the source used by the city's first pipe bringing water to the cathedral. The innovative system was placed in the bottom of a trench and ran from farmland into the city.

As Exeter continued to grow, it became obvious that this first pipe was not enough to quench the city's thirst. In 1346, work started on a new pipe and a well house. A fountain was also built on Cathedral Green. This development had an important new feature: some of the piping was vaulted. This innovative approach meant that the pipe could be accessed easily for repair without having to dig up the ground. But the ordinary citizens of Exeter were only allowed to use a third of the cathedral's water, and so the city decided to build its own pipes. Starting in the 1420s, extra pipes were installed in underground passages that were carefully maintained for hundreds of years. A total of 425m of passages were built beneath Exeter to allow fresh water to reach the city in easily maintainable pipes.

When you're walking around the passages, it feels as if you're going through a tunnel. But that is not the way the network was created. Rather than digging a tunnel, a trench was dug and the walls were lined with stone. Lead piping was laid within the trench before the open space was covered over and manhole covers were added to provide easy access. Lead pipes are no longer used to carry water, of course, because we are now aware of what a health risk lead can be. But lead pipes were commonly used from Roman times right up to the beginning of the 20th century. Another major difference between those medieval pipes and the ones we use today is their size. Pipes made in the 15th century only tended to be 5cm in diameter. Those early pipes also contained many weak spots, so leaks were common and repairs often had to be carried out.

below The passages beneath Exeter delivered fresh water in a project that was technologically ambitious for its time.

35 KENTS CAVERN

EARLY EVIDENCE OF HUMAN LIFE

Kents Cavern sits on a hillside surrounded by a garden of tropical-looking plants, giving it an impressive approach. Swaying palms are what the English Riviera is famous for, although you're unlikely to experience any tropical weather on your trip. When you step inside the cavern itself, however, you'll be within an environment that actually used to be much hotter. The rocks in Kents Cavern were located in the tropics 385 million years ago, and were brought to their current climes by later tectonic processes. The oceanic creatures that died, sank to the bottom of the sea and formed part of the limestone rock are now embedded within a cavern that has been hollowed out and shaped by underground water features over thousands of years.

The Rocky Chamber in Kents Cavern is perhaps the best place to appreciate these geological changes. Water dripping through the cave system deposits calcite, and this lengthy process has produced an impressive array of formations. Stalactites, stalagmites, flowstone, curtains, columns and straws are all pointed out by the guide. It's a very informative

173

above This wooden doorway acts as a portal between the reception and millennia of history.

previous page Guides at Kent's Cavern emphasise storytelling on their tour, engaging young and old alike.

tour, with an emphasis on telling educational stories about what happened in the cavern in centuries gone by.

Before heading into Kents Cavern to see the natural wonders, the tour group is given some historical information in a room close to the reception area. Visitors then head through an unremarkable-looking wooden door in the wall – but therein lies a surprise. When the seemingly normal door opens, it reveals the fabulous interior of Kents Cavern on the other side. You leave the plastered 21st-century reception room and step through into a living history lesson.

The natural formations in this ancient underground landscape are beautiful. But the features of erosion and deposition in Kents Cavern are matched in importance by key historical discoveries made about the early humans who took shelter in this very place. The earliest traces of our ancestors found at Kents Cavern date from around 50,000 years ago, in the shape of flint tools. Humans would not have wandered too far into the dark cave system – but the same cannot be said of animals such as bears. The need to hibernate would have led them into the dark corners of the cave, with their senses enabling them easily to find their way out the following spring.

One of the most significant finds at Kents Cavern was made very close to the entrance door where the tour begins. In the Vestibule Chamber, the jaw of an early modern human was discovered, and it has been dated as being at least 41,000 years old. That makes it the oldest evidence of modern humans to be found in northwest Europe. It also shows how this shelter in the side of the hill was so important to those early humans.

Every twist and turn within Kents Cavern reveals sights that are extremely different to anything you have seen before. The Long Arcade takes you through a dramatic underground canyon; hanging rocks can be spotted in The Labyrinth; and ancient writing is found in the Cave of Inscriptions. One of the most memorable sights is known as The Face, an amazing formation that looks like a human head. Roman artefacts have been found beneath this face, indicating that they may have thought it the face of a god.

Towards the end of the tour, the guide's focus turns to those early humans and what conditions may have been like for them. With prior warning, out go the lights and everybody gets to experience the total darkness of being deep in a cave system. It's impossible to see your hand in front of your face in this 'blackout' part of the tour that has been popular since the 1930s. But then light returns thanks to the guide igniting a primitive type of candle. Evidence of these being used has been found in here, and it's surprising how much light is given off when two or three of them are lit.

SPOTLIGHT

One of the most important Stone Age sites in Europe

Excavation in Victorian times took 15 years and unearthed important historical finds

At a constant 14°C, it's the warmest show cave in the country

Down the years, many famous people have taken this tour of Kents Cavern. Two literary figures stand out because their experiences inside the cavern helped inspire well-known books. You may see works by Agatha Christie in the shop, and that's because a trip to Kents Cavern in the 1920s provided her with the setting for one of her first novels, *The Man in the Brown Suit*, which refers to a cavern where the bones of a mammoth and woolly rhinoceros were found. The name of the underground attraction was changed in the novel to Hampsly Cavern, but it was based on her visit to Kents Cavern. Agatha Christie's interest in the remains found here later developed into a love of archaeology when she married Max Mallowan, an expert in Middle Eastern history. Another famous author to be inspired by Kents Cavern was Beatrix Potter. She holidayed in Devon with her parents. Among many other sketches, she drew the doorway entrance to the cavern. A similar doorway into rocks appeared in her much-loved story about Mrs Tiggy-Winkle, the laundry-obsessed hedgehog.

left High on a hill above Torquay, Kent's Cavern holds clues to how our ancestors lived.

35 KENTS CAVERN

GOING DEEPER...

When William Pengelly moved to Torquay from Looe, Cornwall, in the middle of the 19th century, his aim was to establish himself as a private tutor. He was very successful. Several European royal families took up his services and he was paid for teaching their children. The income he received allowed him to develop his interest in natural history. There are many other caves around Torquay that Pengelly started to explore for ancient artefacts. He discovered bones and tools and established a recording system to show where each one was found.

Out go the lights and everybody gets to experience the total darkness of being deep in a cave system. This 'blackout' part of the tour has been popular since the 1930s.

In March 1865, Pengelly's attention turned to Kents Cavern. He had permission from the owner to explore it and a grant from the British Association. Much of the money was spent on explosives to clear the boulders on the cave floor. An incredible 80,000 objects were found in Kents Cavern over the 15 years of Pengelly's excavation. The important tools found in those fabulous years of discovery include flint spearheads and bone harpoons, along with scrapers and hand-held axes. Animal finds comprised ancient bones of cave bears, woolly mammoths, lions and reindeer.

This important period of excavation stopped on 19 June 1880, marking the end of a 15-year project that had increased knowledge about Britain's early people and that had attracted the attention of scientists all over the world. Bones and tools found by Pengelly's team were sent off to museums in many different countries. You can see a good selection of them at the end of the tour in the Excavators' Exhibition.

Following Pengelly's departure, there was a lull in excavations until the 1920s, when two boys spotted a bone within a crack in the limestone. It turned out to be part of a human skull. When it was removed and taken to London, an expert declared it was 15,000 years old. Excavation work resumed in the caves, and the cavern's famous human jawbone was unearthed in March 1927. This remarkable discovery, which has recently been analysed at Oxford University, showed humans to be living at what was then the edge of the habitable world. It also told us more about how modern humans shared the land with Neanderthals. Kents Cavern is now a Scheduled Ancient Monument: new research can still be carried out, but consultation with English Heritage is needed before any work can be approved.

opposite Mysterious shapes formed over millennia have created an underground scene akin to a fairytale world.

THE LOWDOWN

LOCATION Between Land's End and Penzance, turn off the A30 at Porthcurno

OPENING HOURS Apr–Oct 10–5; between Nov and Mar opening hours vary (refer to website for details)

PRICE £9.50/£8/£5, family £27
ADDRESS Eastern House, Porthcurno, Penzance, Cornwall, TR19 6JX

TEL 01736 810966
EMAIL info@telegraphmuseum.org
WEBSITE www.telegraphmuseum.org

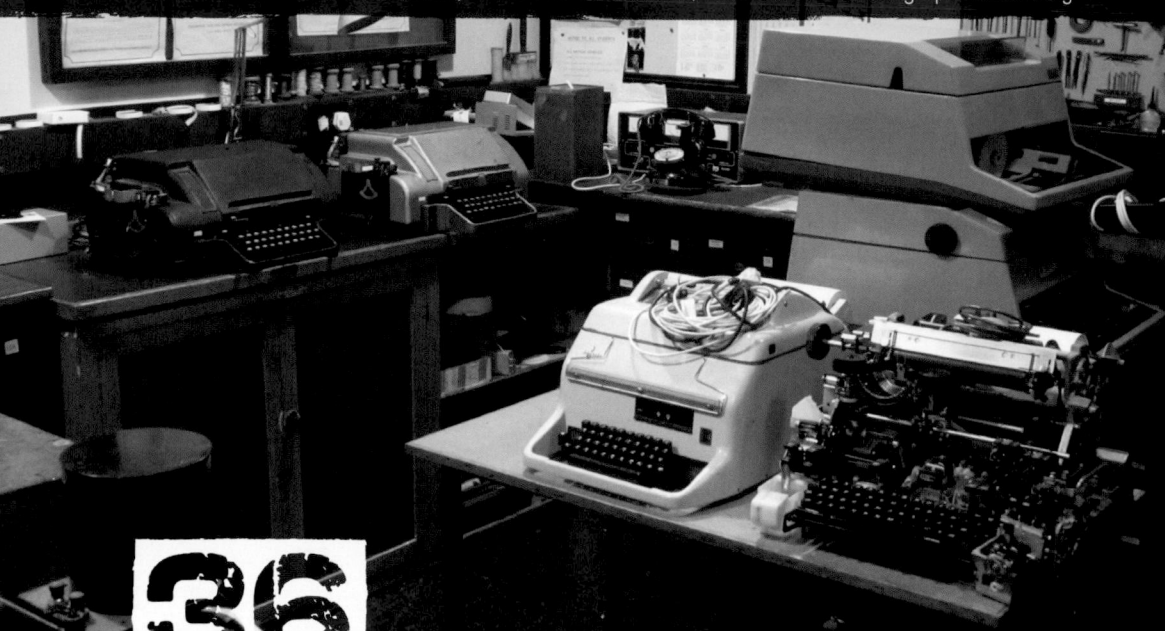

36

TELEGRAPH MUSEUM PORTHCURNO

LINKING THE EMPIRE WITH DOTS AND DASHES

Staggeringly beautiful and off the beaten track, the small coastal village of Porthcurno has several impressive features. There's a glorious beach that's usually comparatively quiet and enjoys serene views of cliffs, waves and boats. The charming Minnack Theatre, eccentrically built into the top of the cliff, provides audiences with the most surreal backdrop to open-air performances. And there's one of the most wonderful museums in the country, telling the story of how this unassuming settlement near the nation's southwestern tip has been at the forefront of modern communications for over a century.

When the British Empire was at its height, fast and reliable messages had to be sent to countries all over the world. But sending overland letters to the likes of India, Singapore and Australia could take weeks. Using cables to send Morse Code messages was much faster and opened up the possibility of having quick replies. An ambitious project to lay communications cables under the sea was begun in the middle of the 19th century, literally connecting places on different sides of the world. Within a few years, cables stretching for thousands of miles were in place. In the UK, they came ashore at Porthcurno.

Suddenly, because of its geographic location and advances in technology, this sleepy coastal community was at the heart of the global communications revolution. Messages – both important and mundane – were processed here and passed on to the intended recipients abroad. Porthcurno's role as the nation's messenger was never more important than it was during the years of World War II, when a tunnel was dug into the hillside to house vital communications equipment and keep it safe during potential air raids. The underground bunker had one simple aim – to keep the telegraph station up and running. The scale of the project is a reminder of how important the cable network at Porthcurno was in allowing the allies to communicate. Another vital job carried out here during the war involved passing on false information to Germans who may have been listening in. To get inside this hillside bunker, you have to leave the main building and follow the sign for the WWII Tunnels, passing a thick blast door on your way in. Although it's difficult to predict what lies in wait along these underground tunnels, most people aren't expecting the sight which greets them. The underground operations room was kitted out with dozens of machines, and when you enter it you'll get an immediate impression of the bustling activity that would have brought this

A charming small village at the heart of the communication revolution

Artefacts from the world's largest telecommunications training college

World War II bomb shelters dug by local miners to protect the important telegraph station

opposite
Communications from across the British Empire arrived in Porthcurno.

below The evacuation route to be used if the Germans invaded.

36 TELEGRAPH MUSEUM PORTHCURNO

shelter to life on a daily basis. Alongside the wealth of equipment, these tunnels also contained many facilities to make life easier for those working here.

This was a potentially dangerous environment as a result of the wartime risk. Flamethrowers guarded the entrances; the doors were capable of withstanding bombs; and preparations were made in case gas attacks became a reality. If the threatened invasion came and the centre was overrun by German troops there was a steep way out at the back of the bunker that would lead staff to a secret exit at the top of the hill. Wandering by the exhibits slowly, reading the information and using the emergency stairs will bring home the reality of what working here must have been like.

The bulk of the museum is housed in the main building, a distinctive white structure dominating the valley. Start off by watching the video upstairs. It gives a fascinating history of Porthcurno's role in global communications and features people who have spent years working here. There are some fabulous interactive exhibits in the museum covering communication through the centuries, including one that gives you the chance to have a go at semaphore. Look out for displays of real telegraph messages, examples of cables that once lay at the bottom of the ocean floor and information about modern fibre optic cables that also come ashore in Cornwall.

below Visitors learn about the village's role in the war as well as the history of global communications.

Save time at the end for a brilliant two-person activity that really demonstrates the complexities of Morse Code and allows people to appreciate the skill involved in sending and receiving those early messages. Two people sit at the opposite ends of a table, each in control of a Morse Code transmitter and with the full coded alphabet in front of them. Each person has to send a message to the other and receive a reply. Nothing could be simpler, you might think. But even if you send the message at a painfully slow speed, the content is likely to get lost in translation as dots blur with dashes and letters are inevitably misinterpreted in a game of secretive Chinese whispers. When you move on and listen to the speed of real Morse Code messages that were sent, you appreciate the immense talent of the operators involved.

GOING DEEPER...

When Cornish tin miners arrived in Porthcurno during the summer of 1940 to begin a tunnelling operation that would last nearly a year, they obviously aroused the suspicion of a few locals. Questions were asked, but the response was clear – there was a shortcut being developed to the local pub. The unlikely tale was intended to throw people off the scent of a major operation that was important for national security. The vital machinery and cables at Porthcurno needed protecting.

Porthcurno's role as the nation's messenger was never more important than it was during the years of World War II, when a tunnel was dug into the hillside.

The decision to move the telegraph station underground was made during the first weeks of World War II. A workforce of 200 miners was drafted in and the £21,000 project began, digging and dynamiting two tunnels into the side of the hill. Two smaller connecting tunnels were made to link these together. A further route provided an exit to the top of the hillside in case of emergency via 120 steep steps painstakingly cut into the hard granite. Working around the clock, mining teams removed 15,000 tons of material from the hillside as the large, windowless workspaces were created. Huge bombproof doors were placed at each tunnel entrance and a military guard was assigned, such was the importance of the communications equipment that was moved in when the covert development was completed in June 1941. This tiny Cornish fishing port was the focal point for 150,000 miles of cable laid along ocean floors. Not surprisingly, camouflage was placed around the secret tunnels to maintain their secrecy.

Communications experts lived and worked inside the underground facility, which had beds, toilets and a canteen. They carried out their duties knowing they were constantly under threat of attack because of Porthcurno's strategic importance. German planes did target the telegraph station during a bombing raid but they dropped their load in a nearby valley, probably believing they had hit the right target. Between D-Day on 6 June 1944 and the end of the war, the subterranean communications centre relayed over 85 million words, passing messages from London to Allied forces all over the world.

<table>
<tr>
<td>THE LOWDOWN</td>
<td>LOCATION Off the B3306 Levant Road, between St Just and St Ives in south-west Cornwall</td>
<td>OPENING HOURS Mid-Mar– late Oct 10.30–5</td>
<td>PRICE £8.10/£4.05, family £20.25, free for National Trust members</td>
<td>ADDRESS Levant Mine, Pendeed, Trewellard, Penzance
TEL 01736 786156
EMAIL info@showcaves.co.uk
WEBSITE www.nationaltrust.org.uk</td>
</tr>
</table>

37

LEVANT MINE

A ONCE BUSY MINE WITH A TRAGIC PAST

As you turn off the road between St Just and St Ives to reach Levant Mine, the scenery could hardly be more dramatic. This former tin mine, which now forms part of the Cornish coast's World Heritage Site, sits on the cliffs overlooking the Atlantic Ocean. It's an extraordinary setting. But it's one that caused plenty of problems for the 'tinners'. During the days when the mine was operational, tunnels and shafts often filled with salt water and needed pumping out. Some of the mining operations were actually carried out under the seabed, far beneath the crashing waves you can see below. As you look north and south along the coastline, other tin mining operations can be seen. It's a reminder of just how important tin mining was to the Cornish economy in the 18th, 19th and 20th centuries.

As you walk down to the entrance, you'll see ruins of old mine buildings on all sides. Most of them were stripped of their contents by scrap merchants following the mine's closure. Fortunately, though, the old beam engine escaped this fate. First used in 1840 and recently restored, the beam engine is operated on certain days to give an idea of how steam power

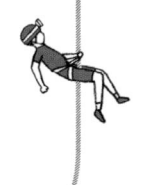

helped the mine in Victorian days. Check in advance to make sure that the beam engine is running before you make your visit. On busier days you'll be given a timed entry to see the demonstration.

The first thing to do after gaining entry to the mine is to sign up for one of the tours included in the admission. They give a comprehensive history not only of operations at this particular site, but of tin and copper mining in general. Both were important here, along with the production of arsenic – a dangerous by-product of tin mining that could bring additional revenues. A common feature mentioned on the tour is how the price of tin and copper fluctuated wildly over the years. The peaks and troughs of their market price had a profound impact on the mining community here at Levant. The workforce in those difficult days could be as low as 30, rising to a 600-strong staff in boom times. Inevitably, the international price of tin and copper shaped the prospects of this community. In the dark days, when Cornish miners were made redundant, they often went out to Mexico, South Africa and Australia, seeking jobs in the mines there. Although tin mining had become economically unfeasible, their expertise

Cliff-top setting of a historic Cornish tin mine operation

Site of a tragic mining disaster in which 31 people lost their lives

Part of the Cornish coast's tin-mining World Heritage Site

opposite The Cornish flag flies proudly next to this remnant of the county's industrial past.

below Many of the Cornish tin mines had a stunning coastal setting and obtained materials from beneath the sea.

was welcome in places mining different minerals. Thus, as the industry in the Southwest declined, Cornish tin miners could be found working all over the world.

The tour at Levant takes visitors through the process of extracting tin from the rocks on this coastline. As well as the mining process itself, you'll learn about the different hammers used by women and children to break up the rock and grind it into a fine material. Tin is heavier than other particles, so it could be easily identified when panning. Look on the internet for the special activity days where the processes are demonstrated to visitors.

Towards the end of the tour, it's time to go underground. Descend the stairs beneath the surface and walk along the long, uneven tunnel to the Levant Man Shaft. This was used to transport men from the surface down to the seam being mined. The tunnel you walk along – around 36m in length – is the same one miners used after getting ready in the 'dry' building. The building itself is no longer there, but look on the floor and you will still see the hollowed-out baths in the concrete that greeted the grimy miners following their six-hour shifts. At the end of the tunnel you can gaze down the shaft and see where those miners disappeared to as they began their work and from where they were brought back up to the surface at the end of a gruelling shift.

below Tours head out from the reception regularly and offer an insightful view into Cornish industrial heritage.

GOING DEEPER...

The Man Shaft ceased operation following a tragedy on the afternoon of Monday 20 October 1919. In a disaster that took the lives of many Cornish tin miners, the link between the engine and rod in the shaft broke. With over 100 men using the man engine at the time, its main beam plummeted down the shaft, killing 31 miners and injuring many more. Many people living in the surrounding villages today had relatives involved in the tragedy. Every year on 20 October a service is

held on the site and wreaths are laid to remember those who went to work and never came home. The shaft was never used again.

The man engine, installed 70 years earlier and in use ever since, operated using a system of moving beams and stationary platforms. The main beam moved up and down the shaft, with steps attached to it at regular intervals that allowed men to climb on and off. The miners were taken up and down the shaft in different stages, getting on and off these plat-

forms that were spaced 12ft apart. Gradually, they made their journey to either the surface or the seam.

By modern health and safety standards, this sounds like a dangerous procedure. And it was. But the use of the man engine was favoured by miners because it was a lot quicker than using the more traditional method of climbing up and down a series of ladders to get to and from the mining face. Because the miners didn't get paid until they reached the rock face, they were keen to get down the shaft quickly. And, of course, after a hard shift in hot, difficult conditions, everybody wanted to reach the surface as fast as they could.

With the man engine broken and debris blocking sections of the shaft, getting the dead and injured out of the mine was dangerous and challenging. Miners from other mines were called for as volunteers were urgently needed to assist. Many came from the nearby mines at Geevor and East Pool. Miners working at Levant who had escaped injury were also among the rescuers. The team worked tirelessly for days until all the dead and injured were recovered from the mine.

The man engine at Levant was never repaired and the deeper levels of the mine accessed by the shaft were never worked again. The mine itself closed 11 years later in 1930, following a collapse in the price of tin. While the commodity had been worth £223 a tonne in January 1929, it had fallen to just £112 a tonne by December 1930. The whole tin-mining industry in Cornwall suffered as a result of this volatile pricing.

THE LOWDOWN

LOCATION On the B3306 between St Just and St Ives

OPENING HOURS Apr–Oct Sun–Fri 9–5; Nov–Mar Sun–Fri 10–4,

PRICE £14.60/£12.50/£8.50 family £45.00
ADDRESS Pendeen, Penzance, Cornwall, TR19 7EW

TEL 01736 786059
EMAIL bookings@geevor.com
WEBSITE www.geevor.com

38 GEEVOR TIN MINE

MINING TIN IN MODERN TIMES

Many people assume Cornish tin mining is a long-dead industry that hasn't employed people in the county for many years. The reality is that some mines in Cornwall were active into the 1990s, producing large quantities of tin. The penultimate tin mine to close was at Geevor. Operations stopped here in 1990, with the pumps optimistically keeping the mine clear of water for another year before they were turned off and silence fell on the once-mighty site. Some of the machinery was cleared from Geevor and sold for scrap in the early '90s, but plenty of the original workings remain *in situ*, meaning that a visit to Geevor is as good an experience of a modern Cornish tin mine as it is possible to have.

The whole visit to this extraordinary place is self-guided, but there are so many helpful employees dotted along the way that it has the feel of a guided tour. They are carefully positioned to talk about the process of mining and answer any questions that pop into your head. And there'll be plenty. The best way to experience Geevor is to follow the suggested route on the map you are given, taking in one part of the tin-mining

process at a time. By doing this, visitors see the story of tin mining from start to finish, beginning with the way workers were transported below the surface and progressing on to look at the methods used to extract the metal from the rock. Thunderously loud machines were used to break up the rocks with steel balls. As the rocks got smaller and smaller they were moved on to subsequent machines until the result was a finely ground material. This was then placed on a series of vibrating racks that sorted out the heavier metal from the lighter rock. Many of these machines operated at once, adding to the industrial noise at this picturesque coastal site as they collected the fine deposits of tin.

Cornish tin mine which ceased operating in 1990 after hundreds of years

Includes a walk through a hand-dug 300-year-old underground mining passage

Tours guided by local people who used to work at the site

Because Geevor was operating into the 1990s, the site contains plenty of modern machinery and has a much more contemporary feel than some of the other tin-mining sites you can visit. But after exploring the more recent processes of tin mining, the underground tour will transport you back in time 300 years for you to appreciate the contrast with how it used to be done. As you wait for the underground tour to start, there is a video to watch and the opportunity to pan for gold, which is just as enjoyable for adults as it is for children. You'll then be asked to collect a hard hat and some overalls from a rack in the building close to the point where you go underground. Putting on the overalls to cover up your own clothes may seem like it's just a gimmick to make you feel like a miner, but when you reach the underground workings, you'll come to realise that it's a great idea. The walls in the dark passageway are so narrow that you inevitably end up scraping the sides in some sections and the overalls protect you from getting dirty. The hard hats are a must; people were smaller 300 years ago and anyone around 6 feet tall will have to stoop pretty much all the way round. Expect a few scrapes of the hard hat as your head catches the rock inside the working area that was known as Wheal Mexico, one of several areas that were eventually combined to form Geevor Mine. The name 'wheal' comes from the Cornish word for 'mine' or 'work', and 'Mexico' is thought to have been added for good luck as investors hoped to mirror the success of Mexican mines. There are no original records detailing when work at Wheal Mexico started, and the entrance to the tunnel was only rediscovered

It was hand-dug out by workers hammering away to gain access to the precious tin resources. Miners working in this way often progressed little more than an inch a day.

right Visitors move from one of the most recent tin mines to one of the first, entering hand-dug tunnels.

previous page Geevor brings the history of Cornish tin mining right up to date, a story that only ended in the 1990s.

in 1995. For safety reasons, the timberwork at the entrance is modern, but the inside remains unchanged.

The second half of the tunnel was blasted out by the Victorians and allows considerably more room to stand in. But the real wonder is in the first part of this underground voyage. It was hand-dug out by workers hammering away to gain access to the precious tin resources. The going was slow; miners working in this way often progressed little more than an inch a day into the rock surface, and the spaces at the face were just about big enough for one man. As workings on these levels progressed further into the ground, broken rock was moved out by wheelbarrow. Experiencing these difficult, cramped conditions for yourself is essential for gaining an understanding of those 18th-century tin-mining operations. Fortunately, there'll be no work for you to complete in there. Instead, you get to chat to the Geevor staff who wait inside the tunnel to guide you through it. At each of these information points, you have the opportunity to ask questions and learn more about how these passageways were used down the years to produce Cornwall's most famous commodity.

GOING DEEPER...

Geevor Tin Mine gives an insight into modern mining methods as well as showing what conditions were like for those extracting metals 300 years ago. The history of Cornish tin mining, though, goes back much further. Even back in the Bronze Age, the land in the Southwest was being worked hard as our ancestors went looking for copper and tin. Throughout the ages, Cornwall has been dependent on the notoriously volatile global prices of tin and copper, and whether you made it rich or endured a poor lifestyle depended on which time period you were investing and working in the tin mines. The most prosperous era for tin miners in the county came in the middle of the 19th century.

During World War II, the demand for tin was at a premium and mining in Cornwall was made one of the national priorities for a government desperate to boost all areas of the war effort. With more men being conscripted to serve overseas, the shortage of miners had a profound impact on the mining industry. By 1941, the government had to take action to stop miners leaving the industry and so introduced the Essential Work Order. Two years later, the Minister of Labour, Ernest Bevin, went a step further in protecting production from Britain's mines. He started the compulsory recruitment of men into mines, with one in ten of every conscripted person being sent underground rather than to battle. They became known as the Bevin Boys, and they worked in mines up and down the country, with over 70 arriving at Geevor.

below Try your hand at searching for tin, watched over by a giant Cornish sculpture.

The fact that Geevor and other tin mines throughout Cornwall represent centuries of significant cultural history was recognised in 2006 when the region was granted UNESCO World Heritage Site status. This puts the Cornish mining landscape on a par with Bath and Canterbury in the UK, as well as with protected places further afield such as Rome, Yosemite National Park and the Statue of Liberty.

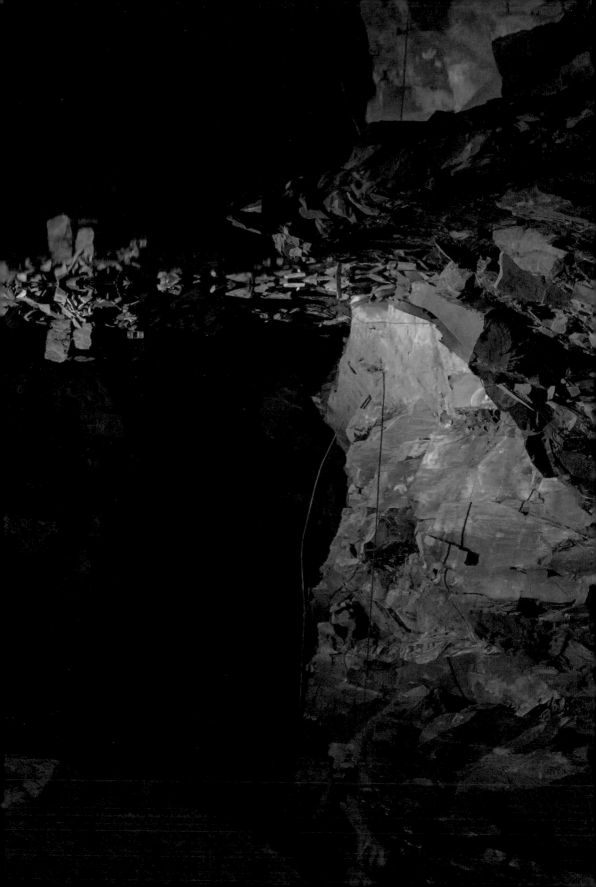

WALES

ABANDONED SLATE MINES
in Wales give adventure seekers
the thrill of a lifetime, as well
as providing an insight into
the working lives of miners
dedicated to getting the nation's
roof tiles out of the ground. Tours
of the Lechwedd Slate Mines take
families on an old mining train
into the depths of Snowdonian
mountains to show how mining
technology changed over the
decades. Take a walk into a
darkened, disused slate mine at
Corris to see tools and candles left
lying around when the operation
suddenly closed. Don a harness
and get ready for some extreme
underground climbing with the
Go Below team near Betwys-y-
Coed, while the energetic family
experience at Bounce Below
will lift you new heights. Round
off your Welsh trip with some
traditional storytelling about
the legendary King Arthur in
a labyrinth of slate formed
millions of years ago.

left Beneath the former slate mines of
north Wales, a wealth of opportunities
await for people of all abilities to explore
to the forgotten subterranean spaces.

CARDIFF CASTLE WARTIME SHELTERS

68

A WARTIME SANCTUARY WITHIN A WELSH ICON

When you buy your ticket for Cardiff Castle, you are gaining entry to so much more than the wartime shelters which kept large numbers of the local population safe during horrific bombing raids in World War II. There are several tours you can book on to when you arrive, including an extensive guide around the house and an insight into how the castle has been used as a film and TV location. A walk around the castle walls is an essential activity, as is checking out the original Roman walls that can be viewed from the back of the shop and café. The high-light for many is the castle keep, still standing proud in the centre of the site after centuries. Photographs on display in the house and online show the keep as an iconic Welsh backdrop for important visits, with everybody from Doctor Who to the leaders of the NATO nations posing in front of this important ruin. As you stand in the centre of the castle grounds

THE LOWDOWN				
LOCATION Cardiff centre on Castle Street	**OPENING HOURS** Daily Mar to Oct 9–6; Nov to Feb 9–5	**PRICE** £13/£11.30/£9.25/ family £38	**TEL** 029 2087 8100 **EMAIL** cardiffcastle@ cardiff.gov.uk	**ADDRESS** Castle Street, Cardiff, CF10 3RB **WEBSITE** www.cardiffcastle.com

and look at the keep, you will see some significant Norman earthworks on the right. Dating from the late 11th century, they slope up to the castle walls and conceal a secret that helped the local population during the difficult war years. Buried beneath here are the passageways built by Lord Bute in the late 19th century that took on a significant new role in World War II as air-raid shelters. Entrance to them is gained by a small door in the embankment, and walking a little way inside will bring you to the long gallery constructed by Lord Bute that was so important during the war.

This wartime shelter was a source of great comfort and protection for the people of Cardiff, even though not all of it is underground. Cracks around the boarded-up windows on the outside of the passageway reveal sunlight. The protection from bombs on this side came from the thick castle walls. Above the shelter and to the left, the earthworks from Norman times gave ample shelter and kept those hiding inside away from danger. On the inside of the passageway, the embankment is many metres thick. Above your head, on top of the wartime shelter, visitors will be walking on the ramparts next to trees towering into the South Wales skyline.

The sound effects within the wartime shelters are striking and extremely thought-provoking. As you walk down the long, straight passage, there are several speakers playing very atmospheric audio clips to give you a sense of what it would have been like in here during the early 1940s. The sound of bombs dropping is loud, the whistling of some of them signifying how they were far too close for comfort, and the terrifying noise of nearby explosions re-creates what those sheltering would have heard. As you press on down the narrow passageway, Dame Vera Lynn sings 'We'll Meet Again'. It's a rousing version with a chorus of people joining in with her, the sound of dropping bombs muffling some of the lyrics. And as you walk further in, Neville Chamberlain can be heard giving his famous radio broadcast from the

opposite Passages in Norman earthworks were an ideal shelter come World War II.

below Sound effects and props bring a 1940s feel to the castle.

When you buy your ticket for Cardiff Castle, you are gaining entry to so much more than the wartime shelters which kept large numbers of the local population safe during horrific bombing raids.

Cabinet Office in Downing Street, declaring that Germany had refused to withdraw from Poland and that Britain was now at war.

Posters from those wartime days are hung on the walls all along the passageway, enhancing the 1940s feel. An old warden's office also has items from World War II on display. The result is a very atmospheric walk up and down a dark passage within the castle that must have been heaving with frightened people on the nights when Cardiff came under attack during German air raids.

GOING DEEPER...

The Roman walls you can see in the castle were hidden from view for hundreds of years. They are now one of the reasons people visit the castle. Behind the café and shop area, you can walk right up to one of the original walls, and you'll also pass them by on the way to the toilet. And from the outside of the castle, as shoppers go about their business and people sit on the grass to socialise and eat their lunch, the Roman walls are clearly visible. As they were being modified and rebuilt, those working on them were asked to put a layer of red sandstone rock around them. It was a clever move that makes the Roman workings really easy to identify.

The reason these historically important Roman walls lay covered up for 900 years was down to the Normans, who built over them with banks of earth as part of their own defensive actions. But in 1888 they were discovered once more when Lord Bute wanted to develop his castle by building a brand-new tower on the east side of the site, along with extending the grounds. When his workmen set about the project, they started to dig away the Norman banks of earthworks, presuming that they were just going to remove a solid mound of earth. But to the surprise of everyone involved in the work, they came across good examples of Roman stonework. At that point, the Marquess of Bute had to reassess the history and origins of the castle and rethink his project.

Bute's initial plans were put to one side following the discovery. He instead decided that all the Norman earthworks on the outside of the castle should be dug away to reveal the full extent of the Roman walls. From 1897, the walls were rebuilt using the original foundations. Although Bute tried to reconstruct the wall as closely as possible to how he envisaged

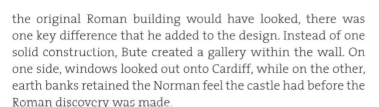

the original Roman building would have looked, there was one key difference that he added to the design. Instead of one solid construction, Bute created a gallery within the wall. On one side, windows looked out onto Cardiff, while on the other, earth banks retained the Norman feel the castle had before the Roman discovery was made.

The gallery within the walls of the castle was created so that access could be gained to some of the original Roman remains. But it was also part of Bute's personal wet-weather entertainment programme. He liked to be able to take his daily exercise within the grounds, and the long, sheltered walkway allowed him to do so even if the rain was pouring down outside. Decades after the galleries were built, the owners of the castle were approached as Cardiff began to prepare for possible German air raids. Permission was given for the galleries to be used as unusual shelters for the local population to take shelter in during Hitler's intense bombing raids. To allow Cardiff residents to have quick access to the shelters, new doors were installed and wooden walkways were built to allow people to reach the shelters quickly from the streets of the Welsh capital.

left Thousands took shelter here in the castle walls, with new entrances giving residents in the capital faster access.

NATIONAL SHOW-CAVES CENTRE FOR WALES

40

THE CAVE THAT TIME FORGOT

At the southern edge of the Brecon Beacons National Park, a brachiosaur peeks its head over the treeline and drinks in what is happening in this pleasant corner of Wales. It's one of over 200 very realistic life-size dinosaur models that are dotted around the National Showcaves Centre for Wales, providing an extra interest for any budding palaeontologists you may take with you. There's certainly more to this underground attraction than what lies beneath; families can also enjoy the playgrounds, farm animals, museums and panning for gold.

However, the most impressive sights you'll see on a visit to this South Wales gem are to be found in the huge cave network that has been carved out by natural processes beneath your feet. Only a fraction of the massive cave system is open to the public. Most of it is only accessible to experienced cavers because of the challenging narrow gaps and the amount of water that has to be negotiated. But

THE LOWDOWN

LOCATION On the A4067 north of Abercraf

OPENING HOURS End of Mar to early Nov 10–3; the cave opens in the local half-term holiday and Christmas

PRICE £15/£12

ADDRESS Abercrave, Swansea, SA9 1GJ

TEL 01639 730284

EMAIL info@showcaves.co.uk

WEBSITE www.showcaves.co.uk

the sections of these caves you can walk through are awe-inspiring. You'll find yourself staring open-mouthed at incredible formations and underground waterfalls. There is a photo opportunity at practically every turn.

Visitors follow a standard route around the site, and the first attraction waiting for you is the Dan-yr-Ogof Cave. The temperature drops noticeably as you enter – and if you visit on a summer's day, it feels practically tropical when you re-emerge into the sunlight. The dinosaurs and associated sound effects certainly add to this illusion! A twisting passage through the caves takes you deep underground, with hundreds of stalactites above your head and some of the most wonderful flowstone creations you're likely to see in the UK. Look out for the calcite creation known as the curtains, along with the tremendous angel – this is actually an example of a thick pillar that forms when a stalactite meets up with a stalagmite on the ground. No guide accompanies you around the cave. You can instead go at your own pace, listening to the audio guides and taking plenty of time to absorb the information imparted to you via screens along the route. It's an amazing journey by pools and stunning rocks, all given an extra dimension with the help of some great lighting.

Perhaps the most fantastic of the three caves is the middle one you'll get to see. Cathedral Cavern is now a venue for weddings. The atmospheric church music played as you enter combines with the impressive lighting to make a tremendous setting for those planning their big day. At the end of the passage, the two stunning waterfalls that cascade from channels up at the top of the cave have to be seen to be believed. They are awesome. Descend the steps and you get to walk right by their plunging torrents. Expect a splash or two as you make your way past them into the large subterranean area known as The Dome of St Paul's. It's here that weddings take place,

The site of a huge cave system, with an extensive network of explored underground passageways

Three different walk-in cave experiences to enjoy

One of the world's largest dinosaur parks, with over 200 life-size models of prehistoric creatures

opposite Prehistoric formations beneath the Welsh hills are beautifully lit.

below When a stalagmite joins with a stalactite, a rare pillar formation is created.

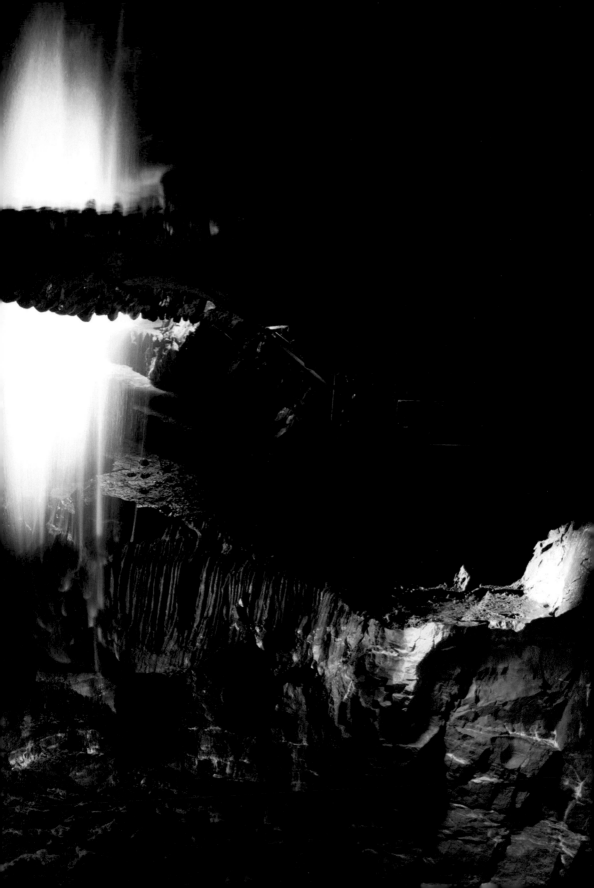

previous pages Cathedral Cavern is dominated by the noise of the waterfalls, yet provides a peaceful space for thought and reflection.

below Weddings can now take place in Cathedral Cavern, where cascading waterfalls make one of the most stunning ceremony settings on Earth.

and the waterfalls make a stunning, unique backdrop for those all-important happy-couple pictures.

By the time you reach Bone Cave, you may well know a great deal about the various dinosaurs you pass. There are quite a few on the climb up to the final cave, where you have to pick up a hard hat in preparation for the low roof inside. Actually, the protective hat seems to be more for the low walkway on the way into the cave; when you reach the passage inside, there's more space above. On the way in, audio features plant a range of questions in your head about why Romans would have been found in the caves, and why bears and sabre-tooth tigers were their previous inhabitants. An excellent short film projected onto the walls of Bone Cave fills in all the answers, providing a very informative history of what went on here in centuries gone by.

GOING DEEPER...

Before you go into Dan-yr-Ogof Cave, keep an eye out for the river Llynfell that flows out of it down to the right. The water you can see in the bottom of the valley – just beyond the dinosaurs – has just taken an underground journey of around 6km and emerged through a passageway into the open air. It's through that narrow gap that the cave network was first discovered by Tommy and Jeff Morgan back in 1912. When they first went into the dark, with only candles to light their way, they had no idea of the fantastic discoveries they were going to make. And heading into the cave as they did was a risky business. They took a rope in with them to help with the climbs, but of course they didn't have a map and they had no idea of the nature of the terrain they would encounter. It was a brave move, and many of the outstanding flowstone forma-tions were discovered by the Morgan brothers on the various ventures they made into Dan-yr-Ogof.

Nothing came close to the discoveries encountered on those Dan-yr-Ogof expeditions undertaken by the Morgan brothers until a caver called Eileen Davies made a significant breakthrough in 1963. She managed to tackle what was known as The Long Crawl – a very challenging squeeze indeed. Once through to the other side, Eileen – who was a relatively inexpe-rienced caver – made startling discoveries that eventually led to a further 16km of cave systems being mapped.

Members of the South Wales Caving Club had already crawled through a similarly narrow gap in 1953 to discover a new series of passages. After blasting their way through some of the rock, they came upon the huge area now known as The Dome of St Pauls. Bone Cave was less of a problem to reach. It was given its name because of the 42 human skeletons found at the back of the cave, the oldest of which dated back 3,000 years to the Bronze Age. Remains of animals have also been found in here, showing it was not just humans making use of it down the years. It is the behaviour of our ancestors, however, that many find most intriguing. A wide range of artefacts have been discovered, including pottery from Roman times, silver rings, bone pins and bronze jewellery. Bone Cave is relatively small in comparison with Dan-yr-Ogof Cave and Cathedral Cavern, but the finds in this particular cave have been quite extraordi-nary. The display at the edges of the cave today reflects these discoveries as well as the competition that existed between humans and animals for safe places to shelter.

CORRIS MINE EXPLORERS

▲ 41

TAKE A HISTORICAL ADVENTURE INTO THE DARK

To experience a unique adventure within an abandoned slate mine and browse a selection of local crafts, set the SatNav for the Corris Craft Centre. You'll find a small village of shops housing a wide array of handmade gifts, from wooden serving spoons to scented candles. At the far end of the craft centre is the meeting point for the Corris Mine Adventure Tours, where you'll come face to face with Mark the Mole, so called because of the amount of time he spends underground. Mark will sort you out with a hard hat, a lamp and a pair of decent wellies. Unless you've got your own waterproof footwear, take advantage of the wellies because it can be surprisingly wet and muddy in the mine. Once kitted out, it's then just a short walk to reach the entrance to the old slate mine where Mark spends many of his days showing people around in the darkness.

Running a range of tours inside this abandoned slate mine and occasionally spending the night in here too, Mark the Mole is a local legend and knows every twist and turn beyond the locked door guarding the mine. It's his expertise that makes

THE LOWDOWN

LOCATION
On the A487 at Corris, Wales.

OPENING HOURS Open all year: tour times vary and it's best to book in advance
PRICE From £13.50/£8.50: price depends on the tour required. not suitable for children under 8

ADDRESS
Corris Craft Centre, Corris, Machynlleth, Powys, SY20 9RF

TEL 01650 517720
EMAIL info@corris mineexplorers.co.uk
WEBSITE www.corris mineexplorers.co.uk

this a memorable thing to do; his aim is to ensure each visit is packed with information and different from any other. To make sure this is the case, he won't waste any time as he moves you between sites. The adventure has a real sense of pace to it. You'll get the chance to ask the odd question, but not too many – there's just too much in here to see and do. To create a unique tour, you'll be asked what type of things you want to see and whether you've already covered any of the places in here on a previous visit. There's also an element of the tour being like a 'choose your own adventure' book from your childhood. If you come to a fork in the path, you'll be given a choice of routes. See a passage off to the left, you'll be asked if you want to explore it. And it soon becomes clear how no two of these underground explorations will be the same. Evidence of the miners can be seen everywhere, from candles placed on the walls to discarded cigarette packets and drinking vessels. In some places the artefacts have been collected together, giving you the chance to have a better look. Some cave explorers may

Expert-led guided tour of an abandoned slate mine strewn with original tools

A range of tours are available, from one-hour tasters to two-day trips that include an underground sleepover

No two tours are alike, heading to different parts of the mine and with the route being varied for returning visitors

opposite You'll have an expert guide on a trip like no other.

below A range of trips are available, from easy to extreme.

be asked to choose one of the items, leading to a story about how it was once used deep underground. This, again, is a way to ensure that every visit varies a little.

Picking the nature of your tour depends on the general age of your group. Nobody under the age of eight will be allowed into the mine, but the age restrictions are higher for some of the longer tours. If you're just after a quick glance at what the mine is like, consider the taster session, which takes you underground for 50 minutes. The two-hour explorer visit goes further into the mine, with longer to bring the local history to life. For those wanting a real underground adventure, go for the half-day mine expedition. This will see you scrambling up slopes, climbing ladders, crawling through holes and using safety ropes to traverse edges. If you're after something even more extreme, call them to see what is available. In the past, the guides have taken groups on multi-day trips that have included a subterranean sleepover and the cooking of a three-course meal many metres below the surface.

The enormity of the slate caverns is quite breathtaking. Huge spaces were cut away by miners over many decades, revealing extraordinary areas that today are a remarkably beautiful highlight of the tour. In one of them, you can gaze up and actually see daylight through an opening high above. A tree grows on the edge of the gap, providing one of the most surreal sights you will see in this country from beneath the ground. This rare source of natural light deep within is at odds with the pitch-black passageways snaking through the rest of the mine. With no electric lighting, you are reliant on the group's torches. And somehow these hand-held lights make it seem as if you are the first person to be discovering the mining artefacts and decades-old graffiti since the doors to this place were closed for good many decades ago.

GOING DEEPER...

The mine explored by underground visitors at Corris is a large network of excavations covering seven different levels. The Corris Mine Explorers have access to levels 4, 5 and 6, though you will only cover a small fraction of the total area on any visit. Part of level 6 is also used by King Arthur's Labyrinth – a tour covered in Chapter 42 – and you can gaze down at some sections of it from vantage points you explore with your guide. The last mining in these hidden depths took place in 1970 and there is a startling amount of equipment left *in situ* by workers who perhaps hoped to return to a job beneath these Welsh mountains one day.

In the golden age of slate mining at Corris, 250 men worked here and earned a wage that allowed them to support their

below and opposite
No two trips into the slate mine are the same. If you've been before, tell the guide and you'll be taken to a different subterranean realm.

families. One of the strongest years on record was 1878, when 7,000 tonnes of slab and roofing slate were mined on this site and dispatched to projects all over the world. Although the first open-cast mining initiatives were established in this area around 1800, it was the arrival of the railway in 1859 that transformed the mine's prospects. Four different mining enterprises had collapsed before the trains arrived, but in 1864 the Braich Goch Slate Quarry Company was established, and production started to expand.

The success of that firm was to be short-lived, though. Falling demand for slate tiles and an increase in production costs led to difficult times and the company ceased operations in 1906. Over the years, others tried to make a go of the mine at Corris. Between the collapse of the Braich Goch Slate Quarry Company and 1970, a further six investors established mining concerns here. The result was an intermittent period of mining throughout much of the 20th century before the passageways fell silent in 1970. A more comprehensive guide to the history of mining in this area is available in a detailed book you can buy at the end of the tour for £10. There's also a Slate Mine Exhibition at the Corris Craft Centre, where you can learn more about local underground operations on a series of information boards.

below Tools and possessions left in the mine show how this was a business that closed suddenly. Workers obviously hoped to return.

LOCATION On the A487 at Corris, Wales

OPENING HOURS Late Mar to early Nov, sailings 10–4.45
PRICE £13.20/£11.40/£8.55

ADDRESS Corris Craft Centre, Corris, Machynlleth, Powys, SY20 9RF
TEL 01654 761584

EMAIL web@king arthurslabyrinth.co.uk
WEBSITE www.king arthurslabyrinth.co.uk

THE LOWDOWN

42

KING ARTHUR'S LABYRINTH

EXPLORE THE LEGEND OF KING ARTHUR

Mysterious boat rides, underground waterfalls and fearsome Welsh dragons lurk beneath the mountain at Corris, all poised to bring ancient stories to life. What was once a slate mine fuelling the local economy has been reinvented as an underground adventure for fun-seeking families on holiday. The mine is dry and a constant 10°C, making it an ideal wet-weather activity for those wanting to get out of their waterproofs. And given that there are plenty of rainy days in this part of the country, visits into the mountain can fill up. Those wanting to enter King Arthur's Labyrinth need to book their slot in advance to secure a place on the boat ride beneath Wales. The departures are timetabled and have a limited number of spaces, so it would be a good idea to get organised and select your preferred voyage online. If you arrive early, the nearby café is a great place to pass some time. Be sure to check out the Corris Mine Explorers trips – featured in Chapter 41 – that also leave from this site.

Gather at the meeting point in plenty of time to make your adventurous voyage underground. There's a shop there where you can buy souvenirs to remember your trip. Just before it's

Former Welsh slate mine innovatively converted into an interactive storytelling centre

Short boat ride takes you beyond a waterfall and into the labyrinth

A tour guide tells the legendary story of King Arthur, aided by models and lighting effects

time to embark, hard hats are handed out and you walk the short journey from the reception area to the mine entrance. Once inside, you meet your guide – fully dressed for the role – and carefully take up your place on the small boat. The channel that visitors sail on was specially created for the attraction and, like the rest of the King Arthur's Labyrinth experience, it helps create a suitable atmosphere for the storytelling and the ancient art of fantastical escapism.

The key moment of the boat ride is the passage beneath the waterfall, a visual metaphor which transports you from the modern era into days of yore. Once you are beyond the waterfall, the stories can begin in earnest. As the tour group is led along the passageways of the old slate mine, several stops are made to look at scenes involving models, weapons and magical creatures. Each of these underground settings, against a surreal industrial backdrop, explores one of the ancient myths connected with King Arthur, his knights, enemies, magicians or armies.

Keep up with the group at all times. It's called a labyrinth for a good reason: the twists and turns in the darkness make it inevitable that you'll become disorientated. Towards the end of the tour, you pass through sections you've already walked through that look completely different the second time around and that now feature different legends. If you're not confused by the layout at first, you will be by the time you're brought back to the boat for the return journey under the waterfall.

Younger members of the group will be enthralled by their time underground as the stories are told in chronological order and much effort is put into creating a land of enchanting wonder. It's not hi-tech and there are no lavish special effects. Instead, all the creativity has gone into this magical exploration of the Arthurian legend. Great use is also made of the vast, sublime spaces that were created by the miners who once toiled down here so that houses around the world could have slates on their roofs.

previous page Models and impressive sets help bring well-loved stories about the legend of King Arthur to life.

Once your voyage of legends has come to an end, there is more to explore on the site. The Lost Legends of the Stone Circle is a simple maze where snaking paths lead to seven mythical stories. A dramatic stone circle sits in the centre of the maze, taking its place in the story as a portal that allows mysterious creatures to visit earth. These enigmatic characters tell their tales amid a landscape of sculptures by artist Stephanie Pasiewicz.

Once you have completed the maze, factor in some time to wander around the Corris Craft Centre, a collection of nine artistic studios. In the small village of craft specialists, you'll find experts dealing with candles, chocolate, pottery, herbal lotions and a range of wooden gifts. You might even see them at work, busy making new products. Try to locate the source of the perfumed aroma as you wander between the shops and you might just find the popular Welsh dragon models billowing out incense. Many of the shops operate seasonal opening hours; you can take a look at what will be open during your visit at www.corriscraftcentre.co.uk.

below Storytellers dress accordingly to impart myths and legends from these ancient hills.

GOING DEEPER...

King Arthur's Labyrinth is to some degree an old-fashioned storytelling experience, though the imaginative methods it employs bring the tales right into the 21st century. The entire visit into the slate mine is wrapped around ancient myths and entangled in legends surrounding King Arthur. The stories are, of course, mysterious and out of this world. But even to this day they are riddled with metaphor and meaning relevant to the history of both Wales and England.

One of the first legends you'll come across refers to a time when the coming of King Arthur was foretold by Merthyn, or Merlin, as he is known outside Wales. When King Vortigan was building a tower to protect himself from invading Saxons, the stones wouldn't stay in place and started falling down. Vortigan was told to spill the blood of Merthyn on the mountains so that the tower would stand. Obviously, Merthyn took issue with this and told King Vortigan what he had seen

below Swords and dragons are at the heart of the tales told in the former slate mine.

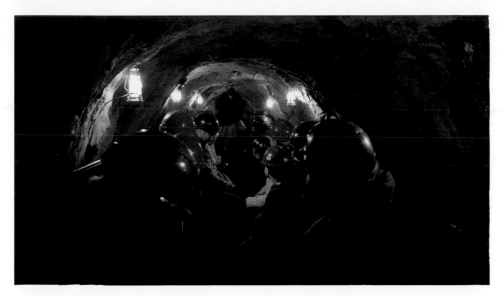

beneath the mountains of Dinas Emrys. He revealed how two dragons had been fighting, one of them white and the other red. Although the white dragon was the stronger of the beasts, Merthyn said that the red dragon would have his day and that a king called Arthur would arrive to drive out the Saxons.

above The trip back in time is made by boat and passes through an enchanted fountain.

Another tale conveyed to visitors is that of Ritta, King of North Wales. Ritta would have instantly been noticeable to friends and enemies alike because of the very distinctive cloak he wore. It was made out of the beards from 28 kings of Britain he had defeated in battle. To complete the cloak, Ritta needed one more beard from one more king. So, when he heard about a new king in the south named Arthur, he took his army to confront him. Things didn't go according to plan for Ritta. His army was terrified by Arthur's weapons and power. But the turning point seemed to be when Arthur pointed out that his own beard was young and there was no way it would cover the hole in the cloak. Ritta's beard, it turned out, would cover the hole and so it was shaved off and added to his own garment. Arthur became the king after the encounter. What happened to the cloak of many beards is uncertain.

Stories such as these are offered at every turn throughout the labyrinth tour. The narrative may seem far-fetched at times, but it is the enduring spirit of these legends that has enabled interest in King Arthur to endure. And with *Game of Thrones* and many similar films proving there are still plenty of fans wanting stories about dragons, ancient armies and giants, the future of King Arthur's Labyrinth looks rosy.

43 BOUNCE BELOW

A SUBTERRANEAN PARADISE FOR ADRENALIN JUNKIES

In the middle of Snowdonia, a former slate mine has been transformed into an adventure centre for thrill-hunters who thrive on extreme activities. Beneath the glorious Welsh mountains, a series of daredevil challenges await fearless folk, and the adrenalin-inducing anticipation begins as soon as you reach the car park. Even before you go inside, the occasional hum of overhead zip-wires will have you glancing skywards at people riding The Titan. Welcome to the longest zip-wire zone in Europe, with three routes seeing passengers fly over 2km through the air. Surrounded by a supreme Snowdonian landscape, this is a place for adventurers run by the adrenalin-seeking company ZipWorld. Two underground activities await visitors deep in the slate mine, the most family-friendly being the jumping feast known as Bounce Below.

The super-springy netted areas at Bounce Below don't have the same feel as a trampoline, though they certainly allow for plenty of time in the air. It's quite a unique feeling beneath your feet, allowing you to go for full-out bouncing or to walk

THE LOWDOWN

LOCATION
On the A470 north of Blaenau Ffestiniog

OPENING HOURS Various time slots during the day; tickets should be booked online well in advance

PRICE Bounce Below: £25/£20, family £75. Caverns: £55 per person (over 10s only)

ADDRESS Zipworld Slate Caverns, Blaenau Ffestiniog, LL41 3NB
TEL 01248 601444
EMAIL info@zipworld.co.uk
WEBSITE www.zipworld.co.uk

from one side to the other like an astronaut in large, gravity-defying steps. A short talk before your bounce time will fill you in on the health-and-safety regulations. You need to wear a supplied hairnet beneath a helmet and should arrive wearing both long sleeves and long trousers. You won't need many layers on, though. The temperature in the cavern is a constant 10°C and the bouncing will soon increase your body heat. Bounce Below is located in a cavern a short walk through a passageway from the Zipworld reception area. There are no toilets apart from those the main entrance, and it would be take a while out of your bouncing session to walk back, so it may be best to make use of them when you arrive. You'll be advised not to take any valuables into the Bounce Below area, for obvious reasons. First, they could get broken if you fall over and land on them, but there is also a risk that smaller items such as car keys could disappear through the gap in the netting, down into the depths below. Fortunately, there are lockers on hand for you to stash your precious things away safely and securely.

The only subterranean playground of its kind in the world, with climbing courses, zip-wires and trampoline-style activities

Bounce Below features a series of huge springy nets suspended in mid-air within an old slate mine

The Caverns adventure includes 11 zip-wires and several climbing challenges

Each of the large bouncing zones is suspended high up in the slate cavern, illuminated by ambient lighting. You can see other people bouncing in sections above and below you, as well as all around. There's plenty of space, though, and the large, enclosed areas never seem to be crowded. The different zones are connected by a series of stairways and slides, meaning you can nip up and down between the various levels easily. It's a surprisingly tiring activity and you'll definitely know you have had a workout at the end of it.

opposite Try to keep on your feet in this multi-layered fun zone.

below Adventurous climbers tackle all kinds of aerial challenges.

Each session lasts an hour, and this can get too much for some people. Not to worry, though, because there's a 'time-out' sanctuary on a solid surface for those wanting a break from the bouncing. The people here tend to be parents who thought they could keep up with their kids' energy levels and have had to rethink their abili-

ties. Although there are likely to be plenty of children booked into your session – especially at weekends and in the school holidays – this is an activity that is also popular among adult groups. If you are taking younger members of your family to enjoy 60 minutes of bouncing, bear in mind that they have to be over seven years old.

GOING DEEPER...

If family members are at least 10 years old and you fancy doing something more challenging than Bounce Below, take a look at what goes on in the Caverns. Occupying the space in the slate mine beneath the suspended, springy fun being had by those bouncing, the Caverns package offers the kind of 'high ropes' experience usually found in the tree tops of a forest. This activity is below the surface of the earth, but you will still be high up, and some of the drops beneath the rope walkways and zip-wires are mesmerising. Atmospheric lighting casts green, blue and purple hues on the huge masses of slate, giving the whole place an otherworldly dimension. Most people will have to overcome one type of fear or another if they are to complete the full Caverns trip.

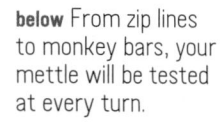

below From zip lines to monkey bars, your mettle will be tested at every turn.

Those taking part are asked to turn up in old clothes and sturdy footwear such as trainers or walking boots. There's a good reason for this – you're likely to get dirty in the bowels of

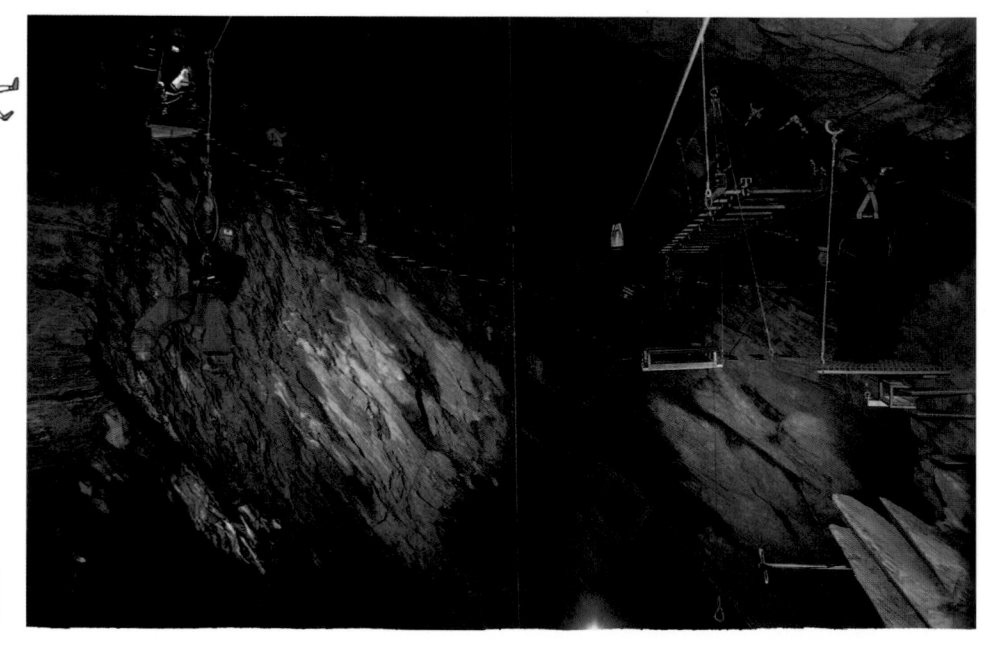

the earth and will need your feet to get a good grip of the footholds. Everything else is provided for you, including a pair of gloves that allow you to firmly grasp the obstacles. A harness is securely fitted around your legs, waist and shoulders, and the zip-wire apparatus is fastened to it. You're now ready to begin your caving adventure. But before tackling the course, there are two levels of training you need to complete. This is something most people will be able to do fairly quickly, but if you do fail the training course you will be entitled to a full refund. The main thing to master is how to use the two 'clickers' that keep you attached to the safety rope during the course. These are very clever pieces of kit designed to prevent any falls. They operate magnetically; once both the clickers are connected to the safety rope, it's impossible to remove both of them at the same time. You can remove them one at a time as you make your way around different sections of the course, but never both together. So rest assured there will always be at least one clicker connecting you to the safety network.

above Lift up your feet and go! Training is given before you embark on the climbing and zip line challenge to boost your confidence.

The obstacles you negotiate are stunning, often with terrifyingly steep drops beneath them. The course begins with traversing along the rock face, before a series of progressively longer and more challenging zip-wires zig-zag the cavern. The second half of the course features a more diverse range of tasks to complete, including rope bridges, scramble nets and ladders. A walkway called 'Islands in the Sky' has metal panels arranged like stepping stones above a deep chasm. An optional extension at the end of the course has what is perhaps the toughest task. With a huge drop beneath you, fourteen monkey bars lead to the other side of the abyss. The safety harness of those not making it across the bars will kick in when they drop, and they can then pull themselves to the other side. An alternative route is available for those who aren't fans of monkey bars, leading to the Stairway to Heaven – a passage up a cliff that needs nerves of steel. A steep zip-wire takes you to the end, where you'll probably want to sign up and have a go at the course again. It's an adrenalin rush in a very managed and safe environment.

THE LOWDOWN

| LOCATION On the A460 north of Blaenau Ffestiniog | OPENING HOURS Book online and arrive 30 minutes before the tour starts PRICE £20, families can buy tickets for £15 each; early-bird tickets are available before 10am for £10 | ADDRESS Llechwedd Slate Caverns, Blaenau Ffestiniog, Gwynedd, LL41 3NB TEL 01766 830306 | EMAIL bookings@ llechwedd.co.uk WEBSITE www. llechwedd-slate-caverns.co.uk |

44

LLECHWEDD SLATE CAVERNS DEEP MINE TOUR

TAKE A RIDE DEEP INTO THE MOUNTAIN

The beauty of the surrounding Welsh countryside is at odds with the gruelling existence experienced by the miners who worked here in semi-darkness back in the 19th century. The hands-on experience on offer here in the heart of Snowdonia allows families to delve into the past as well as into the hillside. You'll attempt some of the working methods they used back in the day and be able to contrast them with more recent mining technologies. After checking in at the reception, you'll be directed across the yard to the meeting area for the underground tour. Put your hard hat on in here and head for the wonderful trains that will transport you 500ft down into the mountain of slate.

Four people can just about squeeze into each of the seating areas on the train, so it's a cosy descent. It's also fascinating to see the daylight disappear and the expressions on faces as you move down into the darkness. These trains were refurbished in 2018 and are part of the oldest and steepest cable railway in Britain. It's a fabulous and atmospheric way to kick off the tour.

The guides showing you round have experience of working in the mine, giving their contributions an added relevance. They will take you around different sections of this extensive underground labyrinth, stopping along the way to give informative talks about many aspects slate mining and the people making a living out of it. The opportunities given to both kids and adults to have a go at mining techniques really help to make the tour memorable. One of these involves children using a long metal rod to create a hole for explosives. A little later, older members of the group get the chance to hoist themselves up the walls of the slate cavern by looping a metal chain around one leg. Mining jobs using this method of reaching the slate ran in families for generations. It was an incredibly painful skill to master during the first few days and there are stories of adults having to force youngsters onto the chain. After this initial period, the skin hardened around the affected area and this means of scaling the walls became more bearable.

In order to complete the tour, you'll have to go down 61 steps, so come prepared for a little physical activity. One of the last things you experience below ground is calm and relaxing, though, as it involves standing back and watching an award-winning and thought-provoking short film projected onto the cavern wall. The setting – a subterranean lake and a church-like underground space – is incredibly atmospheric and enables the arty film about local mining history to fill your senses.

Once you emerge into daylight there's another treat in store to finish the visit off. Roof tiles were the main product made here at Llechwedd. They were used on buildings in the UK and around the world, and in a nearby workshop, you'll get to see how a piece of quarried slate was cut into the shape of a roof

A range of experiences are available, including the Llechwedd Deep Mine Tour

Explores the history of an industry that once had 17,000 Welsh employees

A 'hands-on' trip underground, concluding with an award-winning film

opposite Retrace the footsteps of many Welsh miners.

below The mine is situated in a surreal landscape of disused slate and exquisite mountains.

slate. There's a lot of careful handiwork that goes into prising one thicker piece into thinner slates perfect for keeping buildings dry. You may get to take one of these slates home with you, and there are plenty of other slate products in the shop to browse as well.

The Llechwedd Slate Caverns are a hive of activity. As well learning about the historic slate mine, people come here to take part in extreme adventures organised by ZipWorld. More information about these activities can be found in Chapter 43. A full day could easily be spent here, taking in the slate mine tour and then challenging yourself to an adrenalin-pumping zipwire ride across the mountains before bouncing in the underground caverns. The events are all popular, so it's best to plan what you'd like to do ahead of time and make an online booking to guarantee your slot, whether you're visiting alone or with a group.

GOING DEEPER...

Given that it's a relatively small settlement, Blaenau Ffestiniog punches well above its weight when it comes to its global influence. For decades, the workers in this Welsh town have gone beneath the surface of the earth to get material for a product affecting the appearance of cityscapes the world over. The roof slates made here were shipped to all four corners of the planet, and thousands of buildings still benefit from having Welsh slate on their roof, keeping them dry during downpours.

Mining exploration at Llechwedd began in 1846 under the guidance of JW Greaves, who had experience of the industry at Llanberis. Greaves, who was 29 when he got involved in the slate business, was due to leave Wales on a transatlantic voyage to start a new life for himself in Canada. But he didn't get on board and instead later established a business that has been an important contributor to the Welsh economy. Generations on, a quarry in Snowdonia is still run by his descendants. But two years into explorations at Llechwedd, Greaves became disheartened because of the failure to find any of the slate seams. His business partner left the venture and Greaves himself was facing a real threat of bankruptcy. However, with the project on its last legs, deep slate seams were discovered and the prospects of the region were given a huge boost.

The mine became very profitable and the town of Blaenau Ffestiniog developed as a result. In those Victorian times when slate production was at its height, there were 17,000 men

above An award-winning audio-visual show is the finale of the mine experience.

regularly making the descent into the hillside to bring the raw material to the surface. But the popularity of the slate mining industry was not to last. In the aftermath of World War I, industrial decline and a lack of demand hit Llechwedd hard. Many of the large, hand-dug caverns deep beneath the Welsh mountainside were not fully explored again until the 1970s, when visitor tours began. Some underground mining at Llechwedd continued up until the 1980s, but the scale of the operation never matched those heady days of the 1870s. Cheaper foreign imports and alternative materials took their toll on the mine and on the local community. The main income at Llechwedd now comes from tourism, as visitors from all over the world take a look at where local folk used to work and take part in adventure activities, as well as learning about the origins of slate – how high pressure and great temperatures compacted layers of mud that were deposited 500 million years ago. But the slate story has certainly not ended here. Open-cast quarrying still takes place at Llechwedd and the popular slate is still used to make tiles for roofs, walls and floors. It's even possible to get cheeseboards, coasters and house names made from recently quarried Llechwedd slate.

45 GO BELOW

UNDERGROUND CLIMBING BY TORCHLIGHT

Three different adventurous routes into the Welsh mountains await fun seekers at Go Below. Each has its own difficulty rating, allowing thrill junkies to pick whichever subterranean voyage will whet their appetite and not ignite their deepest fears. Choosing which trip to embark upon could be a tricky task for some people as they try to balance their abilities with their phobias, but making sure you select the right day out for you is the most important decision when you book one of these underground activities. The comparison table on the Go Below website has all the information you need to make a sensible decision. You'll see that there's a huge difference between the basic Challenge and the more demanding Ultimate Xtreme in terms of heights, the number of obstacles offered and the range of challenging manoeuvres. Hardcore outdoor enthusiasts may fancy the tougher traverses, Goliath Zip and freefall jump on the full-day trek for those aged 18+. But the most popular adventure with the highest frequency of departures is the Go Below Challenge, a substantial journey into the dark with a series of relatively hard challenges for those aged ten and above.

THE LOWDOWN

LOCATION Booking office is on the A5 at Conwy Falls, south of Betws-y-Coed; but the meeting point for your trip may be different.

OPENING HOURS Daily; dates and times vary, depending on the tour

PRICE Go Below Challenge £49; Hero Xtreme £79; and Ultimate Xtreme £89

ADDRESS Conwy Falls, Betws-y-Coed, LL24 0PN
TEL 01690 710108
EMAIL ask@go-below.co.uk
WEBSITE www.go-below.co.uk

The Challenge trip sets off from Go Below's booking office building at Conwy Falls, just south of Betws-y-Coed. The other adventures leave from different meeting points, so carefully check the information you'll be sent via email. The kit room near the car park is the first place to head for. Get your name ticked off the list and a pull on a pair of the wellies that are provided before getting your safety harness tightened up. Grab a hard hat and go outside to the minibus for the 15-minute drive out through Penmachno. The journey winds up at the foot of a mountain, where you can see evidence of slate mining on the slopes above you. A 30-minute walk up the hillside leaves you short of breath but also invigorates the soul as the views of Snowdonia open up all around.

Extreme caving adventures deep inside abandoned slate mines in Snowdonia

Led by experienced instructors who also deliver talks about the history of the local mining activity

Obstacles covered include waterfall climbs, air-shaft ascents, ladder scrambles, abseils and zip-wires

When you reach the mine entrance, there's a narrow gap in a gate to crawl through and then you're into the passageway leading deep inside the mine. You'll be thankful for the wellies as you splash your way through pools of water covering old rail tracks that once allowed carts of slate to be transported out of the hillside. This was the route to work for thousands of Welsh miners – some as young as ten – who made a living here over many decades. Because of the long shifts that were worked every day, it was a way of life that meant many did not see any daylight at all in the shorter days between November and March.

The first obstacle to overcome is a crystal-clear and very deep underwater lake. It's the kind of Hobbit-like scene you can imagine Gollum entering at any moment. After donning a life jacket, you climb into a boat that you help your group to row across the water, as you gaze up at the awesome cavern that is lit only with the beams shining from helmet lights. Another body of water, well beneath the surface, needs crossing soon after. This one is navigated with a zip-wire. Everybody has to launch themselves across the gap to get to the passageway at the other side.

above Part of the adventure is made by boat.

opposite Some of the climbing challenges are not for the faint hearted.

45 GO BELOW

Two safety ropes, each connected to a clip – a mechanism known as cowstails – comprise your principal safety device as the climbing challenges begin. By keeping yourself connected to the pre-laid ropes, you're not in danger of falling, even though the sheer drops on some of the route will still lead to an adrenalin rush and cause some folk to back out. Instructions are given for each of the underground challenges in a very clear manner to ensure you don't put a foot wrong. When it's time to rope-climb up a waterfall cascading down the slate, you'll already be confident at using the equipment. A brief break in the middle of the mine gives you the rare chance to enjoy a picnic beneath the surface, so be sure to pack some snacks in your backpack for a darkly lit lunch.

The last task involves climbing up a ventilation shaft that's just short of 100ft deep, using a ladder built into the rock and leaning back on your line of rope to make the ascent easier. Your goal is the small square of sky visible at the top of the shaft, and you emerge from a completely different part of the mine to where you entered, at the end of an exhilarating journey through a mountain made of Welsh slate.

GOING DEEPER...

It's possible to go deeper on a Go Below adventure. A lot deeper. The most extreme of the Go Below trips will take you 1,300ft below the surface to the deepest publicly accessible place in Great Britain. There's a big step-up in the degree of tough-ness required for the 14+ Hero Xtreme trip and the Ultimate Xtreme adult-only venture. Both of these packages are all day

below Go Below offers a range of routes, tailoring the challenges to the ability of those taking part.

events and leave from a different meeting point, enjoying the depths of a different mine to the Challenge package. These are a lot more exciting if you can stomach heights and thrills, with a massive adrenalin rush awaiting those who set off on the Ultimate Xtreme. Expect to fly down up to nine zip-wires, including the notoriously huge one called Goliath. At 130m end to end, it's both the longest and deepest underground zip-wire in the world. The 14 traverses on

this venture for those aged over 18 make the three on the Challenge route look like a walk in the park. There are also three abseils and a freefall jump into darkness that will test even the hardiest underground explorers.

The Ultimate Xtreme course was set up in 2015 after five years of planning. At 5km in length, it's the longest underground adventure route of its kind and takes you to challenging obstacles deep inside a slate mine where thousands have worked in the past. The nine zip-wires make up an important part of the route, crossing deep caverns and bringing you to the next section of the course. One of the lines is really steep, so it has a zip seat to enable you to tackle it in more comfort and enjoy the extraordinary view of the cavern as you descend. One of the toughest moments for many people is a freefall drop into the 70ft-deep dark abyss below. You have to get down to the bottom because the route continues on from there. Those who cannot stomach the leap of faith can try abseiling down, but the quickest way is to get connected to the free-fall machine and simply jump! You'll plummet down through the darkness and cold air, but thankfully the kit will kick in and slow you down for a soft landing. It's not for the faint-hearted, though.

above The route can vary and some of the zip lines are set up while you are on the way around the mine.

45 GO SLOW

225

GREAT ORME MINES

49

A LABYRINTH OF PREHISTORIC PASSAGES

Getting to the Great Orme Mines can be an adventure in itself. You could drive to the top of this prominent hill in North Wales, but there are more exciting options for reaching the site of the mine. The first is to set off on foot from the seafront at Llandudno and walk up the steep slope towards the summit. It's a tough slog, make no mistake. But you'll be rewarded with the fine views that gradually open up with each step and an amazing sense of achievement before you buy your entry ticket. The Great Orme Tramway provides a gentler ascent up the hill, and there are also far-reaching vistas to be seen from the Llandudno Cable Car. Both these alternatives are accessed in the town and are well signed. If you do take a car up Great Orme, follow the signs rather than relying on a SatNav because it may take you the wrong way at the end of the journey.

Before you walk out to the mines themselves, allow time to explore the small exhibition housed in the same building you buy your ticket in. It very effectively sets the scene for your walk around the mines, providing historical context for the pioneering work carried out here thousands of years ago. You'll

THE LOWDOWN

LOCATION On the summit of Great Orme in Llandudno

OPENING HOURS Mid-Mar to early Nov 9.30–4 (last entry)
PRICE £7/£5, family £20

ADDRESS Great Orme Mines, Pyllau Road, Llandudno, LL30 2XG
TEL 01492 870447

EMAIL info@gomines.co.uk
WEBSITE www.gomines.co.uk

also learn about the site's more recent history, notably when the key archaeological discoveries were made that led to the area's conservation.

SPOTLIGHT

4,000-year-old copper mines that are one of the most significant archaeological discoveries of modern times

Thought to be the largest prehistoric mine discovered anywhere in the world

The Bronze Age site was only uncovered in 1987 during a scheme to landscape the Great Orme limestone headland

Once outside, you emerge in an area overlooking the mine complex. It's a great vantage point and allows you to understand the confined area in which people were working. Of course, much of the mine is way below your feet and so hidden from view. There are no fewer than nine levels of Bronze Age mines here on Great Orme, but only the top two are visited on this self-guided tour. The series of cramped tunnels that interconnect and lead away in different directions are sometimes so small that they must have been worked by children. Many of these extremely confined spaces in this multi-storey mining labyrinth are kept off-limits for 21st-century tourists. The key thing to remember is that the tunnels themselves would once have been solid veins of copper ore. The early miners, arriving here 4,000 years ago, would have followed the veins into the hillside and not wasted their time extracting material that wasn't useful.

Visitors will need a reasonable level of fitness to negotiate these ancient mines. There are steps to go up and down, with a

opposite Families can retrace the steps of miners 4,000 years ago.

below The Bronze Age site was hidden until excavations took place in the late 1980s.

46 GREAT ORME MINES

significant level of stooping being required as well. The underground conditions demand a high level of concentration even today, but much more so for the prehistoric people working here four millennia ago, who would have laboured in an extremely difficult environment. The sole source of light would have been provided by candles made from animal fat, resulting in poor visibility and foul smells. And the job of digging out the copper ore had to be done with rocks and animal bones – some 35,000 bones have been found during digs in the last 20 years. The primitive nature of these early tools makes the scale of the achievement staggering. One of the chambers is thought to be the longest example of a prehistoric mining tunnel anywhere in the world.

When you arrive at ground level again after exploring the maze of tiny passages, there's a film to watch about the exploration of the site and some of the artefacts that have been discovered. Information boards around the perimeter of the mines allow you to learn more about their history while gazing down on them from a fantastic vantage point. After leaving the Great Orme Mines, the summit of the Great Orme is a short walk away; if you're able to reach it, you'll get a great 360° view of North Wales and the sea before returning to the town.

GOING DEEPER...

The first mining at the Great Orme took place around 4,000 years ago, but there was no need to dig underground tunnels at first. Malachite, a green-coloured copper ore, could be seen on top of Great Orme. This allowed the first mining operations here on the hill to be open cast. The copper ore was taken from the surface extensively by those early dwellers. Once the easily accessed copper was exhausted, the miners tracked the ore into the ground. Using animal bones and basic tools made from stones found on the beach, the nine levels of Great Orme mines were slowly dug out.

Plenty of waste rock would have been collected along with the copper ore. The physically challenging process of pounding and crushing this would have broken the copper down into smaller fragments. Hand sorting the material then allowed the ore to be separated from the rock. But copper on its own is not a robust metal. As it is relatively soft, experts suggest it would not have had many advantages

> The sole source of light would have been provided by candles made from animal fat, resulting in poor visibility and foul smells. And the job of digging out the copper ore had to be done with rocks and animal bones.

over the readily available local rock. But when a 10% mix of tin is added to the copper, the result is the much stronger and more useful metal we call bronze. Molten bronze was poured into moulds, meaning it could be used to produce a range of valuable tools and weapons.

The most remarkable factor to consider about this first industrial revolution is that the nearest source of tin was 300 miles away in Cornwall. A treacherous sea journey on boats carrying large amounts of material would have been needed for any trade to have taken place. But the contact between those early people living in Cornwall and North Wales was only the tip of the trading iceberg. Bronze axes made here in North Wales 3,500 years ago using Great Orme copper have been found in great quantities over in France and the Netherlands. Bronze Age boats have been discovered in Britain measuring up to 12m long and capable of carrying up to two tons of ore and metal products. Many voyages across the English Channel would have been made as the early civilisation in Llandudno developed and moved forward.

above Visitors take time to stare in wonder along the prehistoric tunnels that were hand-dug to follow the copper deposits.

Exactly how copper ore was first identified on the hillside and known to be of enormous significance may never be known, just as we may never discover the trigger for mixing copper with tin to make bronze. But the importance of these advancements cannot be overstated. The actions of those North Wales pioneers moved society forward in leaps and bounds once it became possible to develop a range of strong metal tools and weapons. Broken implements could be melted down again and remade into something else in an early form of recycling. Whoever was in charge of the copper mines on Great Orme, one of the most important economic and military resources in Europe, would have enjoyed a significant amount of power 4,000 years ago.

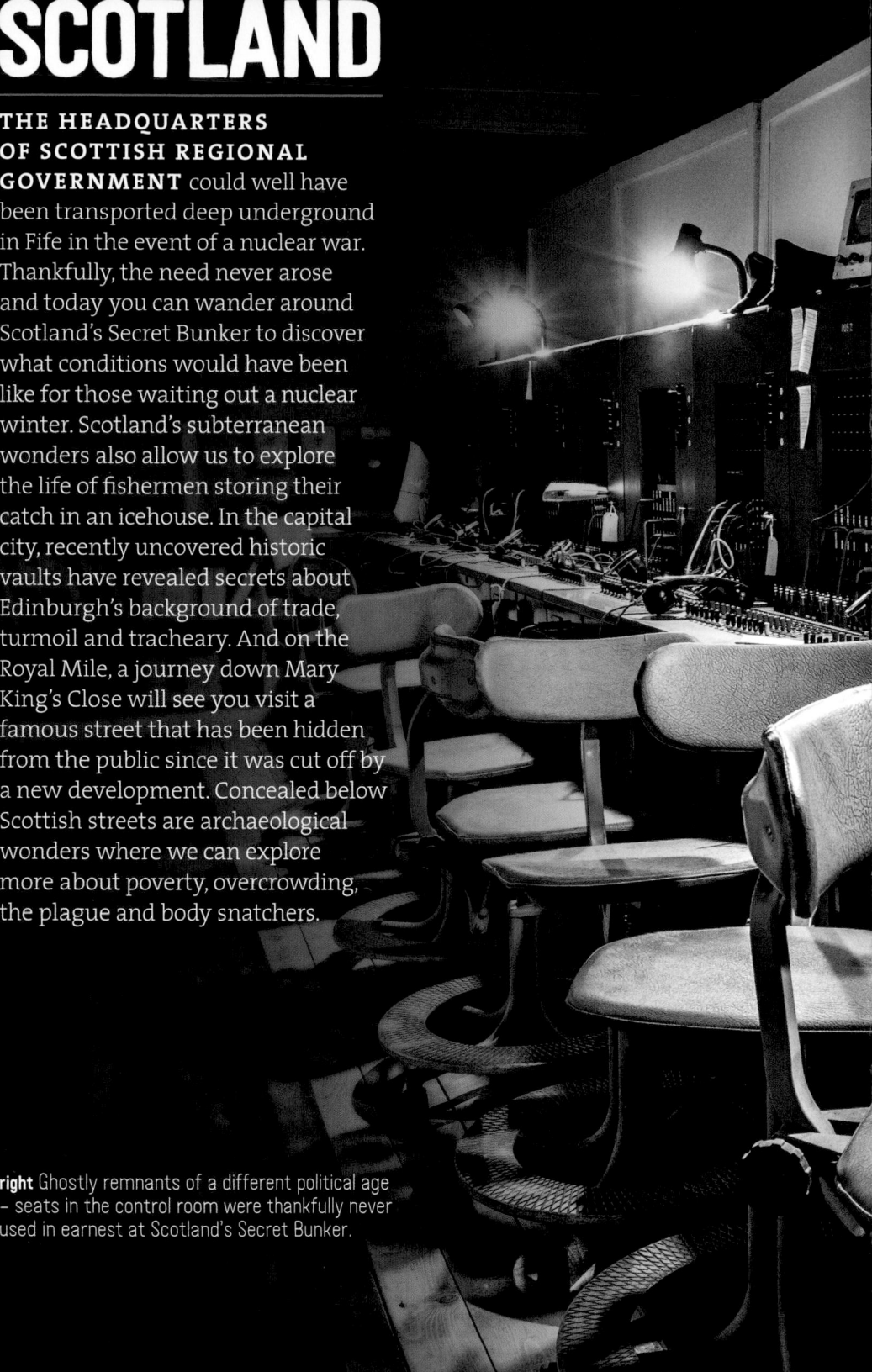

SCOTLAND

THE HEADQUARTERS OF SCOTTISH REGIONAL GOVERNMENT could well have been transported deep underground in Fife in the event of a nuclear war. Thankfully, the need never arose and today you can wander around Scotland's Secret Bunker to discover what conditions would have been like for those waiting out a nuclear winter. Scotland's subterranean wonders also allow us to explore the life of fishermen storing their catch in an icehouse. In the capital city, recently uncovered historic vaults have revealed secrets about Edinburgh's background of trade, turmoil and tracheary. And on the Royal Mile, a journey down Mary King's Close will see you visit a famous street that has been hidden from the public since it was cut off by a new development. Concealed below Scottish streets are archaeological wonders where we can explore more about poverty, overcrowding, the plague and body snatchers.

right Ghostly remnants of a different political age – seats in the control room were thankfully never used in earnest at Scotland's Secret Bunker.

47

THE REAL MARY KING'S CLOSE

IN THE FRIGHTENING FOOTSTEPS OF THE PLAGUE DOCTOR

There is no 'fake' Mary King's Close. The tour you embark on is named The 'Real' Mary King's Close because the guides pride themselves on delivering only factual information to those in their group. What you'll hear is the genuine story of what went on in the streets and rooms that have been hidden beneath Edinburgh's historic Royal Mile for hundreds of years. If something hasn't been proved or is speculation, it won't be included. After all, there is so much we know for sure about this remarkable close in Edinburgh that an hour is hardly enough to cover it.

Mary King's Close was one of the many routes leading off Edinburgh's famous High Street spine. When the tall buildings were constructed around the narrow street, their many floors reflected the social order of the city. With people throwing human waste and litter out of their windows at night, nobody wanted to live at street level, so the wealthiest folk were to be found away from the filth on the upper levels, leaving the accommodation lower down to the poorer people. By the 1750s,

THE LOWDOWN

LOCATION On Edinburgh's Royal Mile, opposite the Mercat Cross

OPENING HOURS Apr–Oct 10–9, Nov Sun 9.30–6.30, Mon–Thurs 9.30–5.30, Fri/Sat, 9.30–9. Dec– Mar Sun–Thurs 10–5, Fri/Sat 10–9

PRICE £15.50/£13.50/£9.50, family £42.50; not suitable for under 5s

ADDRESS 2 Warriston's Close, High Street, Edinburgh, EH1 1PG

TEL 0131 225 0672

EMAIL contact@real marykingsclose.com

WEBSITE www.real marykingsclose.com

many buildings were in a poor state and city leaders wanted to get traders off the street into a new trading area. The tops of the buildings around Mary King's Close were cropped off and vaulted ceilings were created to strengthen the foundations so that a new Royal Exchange could be constructed on top of them. In the end, few traders were interested in moving inside the Royal Exchange and instead remained as street sellers. In 1811, the council gave up on its plan and acquired the Royal Exchange for itself. It's now known as the City Chambers, and it still stands just below the entrance to The Real Mary King's Close.

An hour-long tour taking you below the current street level in the heart of Edinburgh

Informative look at the city's history provided by a costumed guide, focusing on living conditions and the plague

A social history tour around the base of early tenement buildings hailed as the world's first skyscrapers

Several of Edinburgh's narrow closes were shut off and covered over to make way for the new building, but part of Mary King's Close remained vibrant. Glovers, wigmakers, engravers and merchants were all still thriving here at the end of the 18th century. A family of sawmakers called the Chesneys moved into the close during 1850. Soon after, however, the council started buying up land so that it could expand the City Chambers. Andrew Chesney refused to move until he was forced to go at the turn of the 20th century.

opposite Guides stick to the real facts and don't speculate about the past.

below Passages beneath Edinburgh were hidden away for centuries.

The Chesney workshop can still be seen on the tour. An upward glance would once have provided anyone standing outside the workshop with a glimpse of blue sky above the multistorey tenements. Today, however, it is a good place from which to see the City Chambers above and appreciate how the buildings were cut off and built over. The enclosed space gives this historic street the feel of a museum, but this is no reconstruction.

There are so many hidden gems on this tour that it's quite hard to take it all in; whenever your guide stops, you'll find yourself in a space steeped in history with a distinct link to Edinburgh's past. On Allan's Close, there is a group of rooms that have survived from the 17th century. Experts have dated the earliest

features of the room to 1640. Although they now look weary and worn, this is a fascinating insight into the homes people lived in at around the time of the plague. Parts of the original fabric have been found in these rooms, and some of the plaster is covered by 250-year-old printed decoration.

A particularly humbling part of your wander around Mary King's Close involves learning about the suffering of its residents when the plague struck in 1644. Scotland was no stranger to outbreaks of plague over the centuries but this episode – which was to be the last – was particularly horrific. Many wealthy residents fled the city at the first sign of the outbreak. The people left behind were soon threatened with punishment if they tried to follow. Life started to grind to a halt. Business slowed, schools were closed and Parliament left Edinburgh. A huge effort was made to care for the sick and disinfect the homes of those affected, which could include burning their belongings. Those suspected of having the infection were put into quarantine for up to six weeks. They had food, ale and coal delivered every day and only came out when their period of quarantine was over. Or when they died.

Several of Edinburgh's narrow closes were shut off and covered over to make way for the new building, but part of Mary King's Close remained vibrant. Glovers, wigmakers, engravers and merchants were all still thriving here.

Lifelike models of the sick in these former dwellings bring home the suffering and how families were ripped apart. Most haunting is the replica of the visiting doctor, dressed in his plague outfit that was intentionally frightening to scare away the bad spirits. A thick coat, gloves and hat protected their body and a bird-like mask was filled with spices and flowers so that they did not have to smell infected and rotting bodies. When you climb steep steps and arrive at the present-day Royal Mile once more, there is a coffee house nearby where you can reflect on all you've learnt. Look out for the large painting of a plague doctor hanging on the wall, the most poignant image from this journey into Edinburgh's past.

GOING DEEPER...

The street that was to become known as Mary King's Close was originally called Alexander King's Close. Alexander was not related to Mary, but the fact that they shared the same surname is thought to be one of the reasons why the name of the passage was eventually changed to Mary King's Close. The other factor was that Mary King, born at the end of the

opposite The buildings were tall because of the limited space with the city walls.

16th century, was a successful trader and a colourful local character. It was very unusual for streets to be named after women in those days, but the hard-working Mary King was clearly a memorable resident in the close.

Not a great deal of information is known about Mary King and research is still ongoing, but records have been found of her marriage to local merchant Thomas Nemo in 1616. The couple had four children, but Thomas died in 1629. This left Mary King with the difficult task of bringing up their children alone; soon after she moved onto the close that would eventually bear her name. In 1635, a document was drawn up for tax purposes which had the names of all the landlords and tenants in the closes of the Royal Mile. Mary King rented a turnpike house with a cellar and also a shop on the High Street, paying a high rent for it because of its prominent position opposite the Mercat Cross. From here, Mary King traded fabrics and made a comfortable living. She died in 1644, and her last will and testament paints a picture of what she had accumulated during her lifetime. Among her possessions were two gold rings, six silver spoons, three buffet stools, over 60 cushions and pillows, ten spools of sewing thread and nine dozen table napkins. In the years following her death, the street became known as Mary King's Close, and thanks to the way the City Chambers were developed, a key part of the city's heritage has been preserved.

below A model of the site gives a perspective it's hard to gain when you're inside the dark passages.

48 EDINBURGH'S BLAIR STREET VAULTS

WALK THROUGH THE HAUNTS OF THE BODY SNATCHER

These tours of underground Edinburgh meet by the Mercat Cross on the Royal Mile. Nothing to do with furry little animals, a mercat is the old Scottish name for a market, providing the inspiration for Mercat Tours' name. Planning your guided historical experience in Edinburgh should ideally start well before you get to the Scottish capital as this company offers so many different tours that time is needed to explore its website and find the right one for you. There is more than one kind of underground tour that explores the vaults on Blair Street. Some are historical tours that run during the day, but there are also ghost tours at night for the over-18s, so make sure you book a tour that's suitable for your particular group.

Before you actually head underground, there are sights to see above the surface as you start to appreciate the city's history. The main thing to try and

Storytelling walking tours that meet on Edinburgh's Royal Mile and explore the city's history

The underground trips have exclusive access to the Blair Street Vaults beneath the Old Town, which hold gruesome secrets

These vaults were initially home to tradesmen, but families also lived there in cramped conditions

previous page The Edinburgh vaults are chilling, mysterious and dark.

below Guides dress for the part on some of the more scarier adventures below the capital.

get your head round as you try to understand life hundreds of years ago is that Edinburgh was a much smaller place back then. The city revolved around the Old Town now known as the Royal Mile. A lake stood to the north in what is now Princes Street Gardens and an unpleasant area of slums was located down the other side of the hill towards Cowgate. Your guide will show you maps of the city at different periods to give you some historical context for the tour.

Some of the passageways leading away from the Royal Mile make ideal places to stop and listen to stories of days gone by. Many of these passages are called 'closes', such as Anchor Close, because they could be closed off at night to keep people out. In the 18th century, all had one thing in common – they contained buildings with a large number of storeys. The reason Edinburgh was home to these skyscrapers of the day was down to the protective wall surrounding the Old Town.

Edinburgh's city walls were designed to keep out hostile English forces, but they had the imprisoning effect of keeping

Scottish people trapped within the confines of the city. Many people did not leave Edinburgh at all, mainly because they were poor and would have to pay a charge for re-entering. With space for further development within the all-important walls being extremely limited, the answer was to build upwards. Rooms were built upon rooms until there were often ten storeys to these early buildings. Overcrowding was rife, hygiene was poor, and residents threw their excrement out of their windows. Living conditions were grim.

below Tours meet in the heart of the old town and enjoy some historical information about Edinburgh before heading underground.

The tour takes you to Cowgate, where the roadside filth was so great that people used to wear shoe covers to avoid getting dirty. The wealthiest folk could hire a sedan chair from the Royal Mile to cross Cowgate without encountering the unpleasantness below. In 1788, Edinburgh's South Bridge took Cowgate out of the equation. It allowed people to move from the Royal Mile out towards the university district to much better conditions, leaving the unhealthy grime behind. The 19-arch structure contains dozens of vaults that were originally used by craftsmen wanting to take advantage of the footfall on the bridge and sell their wares.

The tour enters these dark underground areas that are atmospherically lit by dozens of candles. Visitors may choose to use torches on their phones to help them move between the vaults as the floor can be uneven and the amount of light is very limited. Each of these subterranean spaces has a historical tale associated with it, told in an often-chilling manner by your guide. And you don't have to look far for history you can touch – the floor in some areas is littered with oysters and glass from 18th-century wine bottles, while shelves that had been converted into beds for poor families remain.

People working in the vaults in times past would have experienced harsh conditions, not least having to put up with the smell of human waste mixed with the odours from sweat and candles made from animal fat. But there was time for at least some fun down here. The final room you visit contains items found when the vaults were excavated in the 1980s, among which is a glass pistol. These were typically won in local fairs and would have been filled with sweets. It's a heartening insight into a childhood which would have ended at around the age of five, when many youngsters were sent out to work.

GOING DEEPER...

The vaults below the South Bridge were some of the most desirable properties in Europe when they were built in 1788, and they had a price tag to match. Shops on the surface benefited from a good level of passing trade as people moved between the city centre and the university district. The vaults lying beneath ranged in size from two to forty square metres and were used as both workshops and storage areas to service the shops above. But things didn't go as planned down below. The bridge was built quickly, and the design did not feature any waterproofing layers near the surface. With Edinburgh's weather being notoriously wet, it did not take long for dripping water to become a real problem deep down in the vaults. Damp conditions made it hard for some craftsmen to make their goods, while flooding, muddy floors and seeping sewage made these dark spaces unwanted. By 1820, many of the shoemakers, cutlers, engravers and watchmakers had moved out.

The floor in some areas is littered with oysters and glass from 18th-century wine bottles, while shelves that had been converted into beds for poor families remain visible today.

These hidden empty vaults took on more sinister roles in the early 19th century. Crime became commonplace here and one area was even used as an illegal whisky distillery. The most notorious criminals to operate in the vaults were body snatchers. After digging up freshly buried corpses in nearby churchyards, these dubious tradesmen would then carry their

loot up to the university, where the bodies would be used in lectures and for research. The passages beneath the South Bridge provided an ideal route for the clandestine operation. Bodies dug up one night were often stored here to be moved the following evening.

Some of the smaller rooms in this underground labyrinth became slum dwellings. It's almost unimaginable today, but families with as many as ten members would reside in some of the smallest underground spaces you'll see on the tour. It was an unhealthy lifestyle which resulted in a very low life expectancy. During the 19th century, most of the vaults were emptied and the entrances were filled with rubble to prevent flooding and to stop squatters moving in. The hidden world below the street level of South Bridge remained lost for over 100 years. Then, in the early 1980s, the owner of a bar on the bridge discovered part of the underground network of vaults and slowly started to clear rubble out of the chambers by hand. The process took Norrie Rowan years to complete and revealed many artefacts along the way – some of which are now on display at the end of the tour.

above From damp walls to glass bottles and oyster shells under your feet, the social history of Edinburgh is literally all around you.

49

SCOTLAND'S SECRET BUNKER

A PLACE TO SHELTER FROM NUCLEAR TERRORS

The countryside surrounding Scotland's Secret Bunker seems a million miles away from the horrors associated with the threat of World War III and a nuclear winter. A few miles to the north, the bustling university town of St Andrews welcomes students and golf lovers alike. A short drive south brings you to an outstanding coastline stretching down towards Kirkcaldy, with views over the Firth of Forth. But between the 1950s and the early 1990s, this site was preparing for just such an event that would have rendered Scotland's scenic links irrelevant. From the outside, this nondescript building has the appearance of a family home. But it houses a deep secret. Descend the stairs inside and you're soon surrounded by eerie scenes that could be a set from a Cold War thriller. But this was not built for a film. This was constructed for what was very nearly the greatest drama in history.

Your walk down the long tunnel leading to the bunker is made even more chilling by the chatter of people that you can hear through speakers as you approach. If this journey had ever actually been made in earnest by those working here, it would have meant that the four-minute-warning had been given and life as we know it would have ceased. At the end of the tunnel, huge red blast doors stand open as you pass them – but these would have been shut tight if the worst had happened. Once you are in the bunker, from this point of entry, there is at least 10ft of solid concrete above your head.

Off the main corridor, there are a number of different rooms to explore. Some you can peer into, some you can actually go in, and some are locked. It's worth trying all the door handles and reading the signs on them to make sure you are going into all the areas you are allowed access to. One of the best rooms on this level is the dormitory. With hard bunkbeds down each side of the large room and numbered lockers standing next to each one, this room has character that is boosted by a radio broadcast from the Cold War days that is played through speakers.

Another door to look out for leads into the radio room. With antiquated equipment still set up and looking as if it could be used at any moment, this is where emergency broadcasts would have been transmitted to a population trying to survive and no doubt scared to death. You can listen to examples of these broadcasts, which inform people about what to do during the imminent explosion and how to deal with fallout in the coming days. The passing of time makes the recordings no less terrifying.

The canteen is open from lunchtime, serving drinks and snacks. During the 1950s, when the bunker first opened and the Cold War raged on, the canteen was separated into strict male and female sections, with food served through hatches; the hatches can still be seen, but you are allowed to sit in family groups today! The canteen is decorated in a retro style. As you enjoy a coffee here you'll experience an eerie feeling

A well-kept secret for 40 years before being opened to the public in 1994

Visitors are led underground through a 450ft tunnel and two huge metal blast doors

The bunker sits 100ft below the surface and has an area that would cover two football pitches

opposite The bunker contained the latest equipment at the time it was last operational.

below The dorms provided basic beds in uncomfortable times.

Descend the stairs inside and you're soon surrounded by eerie scenes that could be a set from a Cold War thriller. But this was not built for a film.

knowing that you are deep underground and that those once taking their meals here were trained for an end-of-the-world eventuality.

The unnerving rooms keep coming as you make your way along the top corridor and down the steps to the bottom level. Look out for the operations room, complete with maps designed to track nuclear blasts and plot the course of fallout. Displays in glass cases reveal a range of equipment specifically designed to detect such unwelcome dangers. Perhaps most poignant of all the rooms is the small chapel, which is one of the world's few subterranean places of worship. The organ, cross and rows of seats make it look so similar to a regular church, and yet the ceiling, lighting and door with a 'No Entry' sign make it anything but. Prayers said in here would have been desperate and heartfelt.

GOING DEEPER...

When the bunker was designed, every effort was made to ensure it would withstand a nuclear strike. The survival of this subterranean shelter would have depended on the strength of the blast and how far away it was from ground zero. Construction began with a 125ft hole being excavated and lined with tons of gravel to produce the effect of a shock absorber beneath the Scottish landscape. The concrete bunker was then built within the hole, with thick layers of concrete reinforcing the structure on every side. This concrete layer is up to 15ft thick in some places, with strong tungsten rods inserted into the casing every 15cm to provide additional strength. The excavated earth was then piled on top of the bunker, forming an extra layer of protection in the form of a mound that can still be seen today. Work started here in 1951, but the 250 people involved in building the bunker were not told what it was going to be used for. They also had to sign the Official Secrets Act, making it an offence to talk about what they saw here. Drivers delivering building materials had to deposit their loads away from the construction site, leaving the site workers to load them onto different lorries in order to transport them to where the bunker was being built.

If there had been a nuclear strike on Britain during the Cold War, as many as 300 people could have been accommodated at the bunker in Fife. This would have included some of the most senior politicians and decision makers in Scotland. While

the country was being blown to bits, the bunker beneath Fife would have been one of the government's regional control centres. From here, officials would have tried to maintain some element of control in Scotland and endeavoured to pick up the pieces in the post-nuclear nation.

Initially, the bunker was built as part of the early warning system, with the Civil Defence Corps moving in during 1958 and using it as a regional headquarters for ten years. The bunker was then refurbished and given the job of being the central government HQ for Scotland in the event of a nuclear war. Scotland had three underground bunker control centres at the height of the Cold War, but over time the focus became this site near St Andrews, which was the last one in operation. It had been due to get a major facelift in the early 1990s, but as the Cold War ended in 1991, this was never needed.

After being decommissioned in 1993, the secret bunker was put up for sale and was bought by a consortium of businessmen from Edinburgh. Some maintenance had to be carried out in the bunker to get the site ready for members of the public to look around. Repairs to the floor were made, carpets were replaced and smoke alarms were fitted. But much of the underground complex, including the dormitories and radio room, have been left exactly as they were in the early '90s.

below Scotland's damaged infrastructure would have been monitored from the underground shelter.

THE LOWDOWN

LOCATION East of Inverness, off the A96 at Spey Bay

OPENING HOURS The Centre opens March weekends: 10.30–5; early Apr to late Oct daily: 10.30–5 (closed Nov–Feb); its ice-house tours run at set times – call ahead for details

PRICE Free entry and tour
ADDRESS Spey Bay, Fochabers, Moray, IV32 7PJ

TEL 01343 820339
EMAIL dolphincentre @whales.org
WEBSITE www.dolphin centre.whales.org

50 SPEY BAY ICEHOUSE

SALMON, SALMON, EVERYWHERE...

Tours of the icehouse at Spey Bay run at various times throughout the day and give a thoroughly engaging overview of conservation, local wildlife and how the fishing industry has played a key role in the local economy. There is no need to book ahead for these guided tours and there is no charge for going on them, though you may wish to make a donation to the Scottish Dolphin Centre. For anyone short on time and needing to plan their day, it may be worth calling ahead to get an idea of when tours are taking place. If you have fewer time restraints, turn up as early as you can and choose the tour you want to go on. If you need to wait a while, this is a lovely place to have a walk or enjoy a drink in the café. And, of course, one of the best things to do while you're here is to take the time to spot the dolphins off the shore.

There's a short walk from the Dolphin Centre to the icehouse at the start of the tour, and you'll have a brief health-and-safety talk before you enter. The main points to keep in mind are that the floor can be uneven and some of the doorways are fairly low. Once inside, you'll be instantly drawn to

four stunning mosaics made by children from local schools. Inspect them closely and you'll see that each one is made from beach litter that washed up nearby. Ranging from various pieces of plastic to crockery and gun cartridges, these are as environmentally educational as they are creative.

The icehouse is more spacious than it initially appears, as two thirds of the building is hidden from view when you're outside. From inside, the section that stands over ground begins above your head at the point where the white paint starts. Split into six different chambers, the exhibitions in the icehouse are divided into different themes. The first thing you experience is the Dry Dive. As its name suggests, it takes you beneath the waves without getting you wet. Films projected onto the walls of the chamber bring you up to speed with the wildlife that can be spotted in the area, from ospreys to common seals. A second film takes you beneath the Moray Firth, showing the variety of species in the sea just a few metres from where you stand. Look out for the plastic bags, which have an appearance very similar to jellyfish in the sea. Sadly, marine mammals get them mixed up a lot too, leading to serious health issues when they eat them.

When you reach the tool room, you'll learn more about the building and its use as an icehouse. It was a role that was crucial for the local economy in the 19th century. Ice from local ponds was brought here and the salmon was packed in it. The icehouse was never used as a long-term storage facility. Instead, the salmon brought here could be preserved for up to ten days before being transported to markets around the country. Conditions were freezing, as you might imagine. But the work was hard and the men employed here would easily work up a sweat. It was common for them to work topless, despite everything the icy weather threw at them.

Using a sweep net was the most successful method of fishing for salmon, and in the Victorian heyday of the industry the average daily catch was around 1,000 fish. This meant there

Based at the Scottish Dolphin Centre, a great place to spot bottlenose dolphins

Home to the largest icehouse in the country, built in 1830 and used to keep salmon fresh

Tours bring to life the history of local fishing and how it developed over the centuries

opposite The icehouse at Spey Bay was the central hub of the region's salmon fishing industry that kept London's tables well stocked.

below Inside the icehouse, explore the local significance of several marine species.

50 SPEY BAY ICEHOUSE

was plenty of salmon to go around the country, and London in particular was awash with it in the 19th century. Servants working in the capital's houses were being fed so much salmon that some had a condition written into their contract stating there would be no more than three servings of this fish a week!

Having brushed up on the history of salmon fishing, make sure you save time to explore the surrounding site. As well as being on the lookout for wildlife, you can cast your eyes around a now-tranquil landscape that was once a hectic and vibrant one where workers scurried around trying to complete their chores.

GOING DEEPER...

The icehouse is looked after by the Scottish Dolphin Centre, a charming place where, over the summer months, crowds gather to gaze out and spot the lively marine mammals frolicking in the Moray Firth. The centre is part of the Whale and Dolphin Conservation charity. Although admission is free, donations are needed to maintain the conservation and education work being carried out across Scotland. As well as protecting the dolphins in the Moray Firth, projects have been established to look after harbour porpoises throughout the country and dolphins on the Isle of Lewis.

below Nature fans head here for the wildlife-spotting and return with a sound knowledge of the salmon trade.

Before and after your tour of the icehouse, you should take time to walk along the beach and look out for the playful bottlenose dolphins. They can be spotted most days, and it's worth packing a pair of binoculars for your trip. You're likely

to be in good company as this is a very popular place from which to gaze out to sea in hope of seeing the playful creatures. Information about recent sightings can be obtained at the visitor centre.

This is the point where the river Spey enters the Moray Firth. The Spey is the fastest flowing river in the UK and has been a major source of salmon for centuries. There was a fishing community around Spey Bay back in the 11th century and the fishing industry was crucial to the local economy right up to the mid-1990s. The importance

of the Spey as a salmon spawning ground has long been recognised. As far back as 1400, King Robert III declared that the death penalty would be handed out to anybody convicted of killing salmon three times during the crucial spawning season.

The building housing the exhibition, the shop and the café dates back to 1768, and was originally used as a preparation area by fishermen. Two chimneys leading up from the café once serviced a large fire pit. Inside, look out for the black hoist which was used to move fish from the servicing area to the fire, and then back again. Fishermen brought the fish into this building, where they were gutted, boiled, pickled and 'kitted' – a term referring to how they were packed into boxes.

These containers full of salmon were then moved to the icehouse for temporary storage. This large building, constructed in 1830, is itself like an iceberg in that most of it is hidden beneath the surface. Eagle-eyed visitors may spot the stone on the front of it which suggests it was built in 1630, but don't be fooled by this as it was probably reclaimed from a different local building. Several nearby structures were damaged in severe floods that hit the area in 1829; the dating stone and other building materials may have been brought from these ruins the following year.

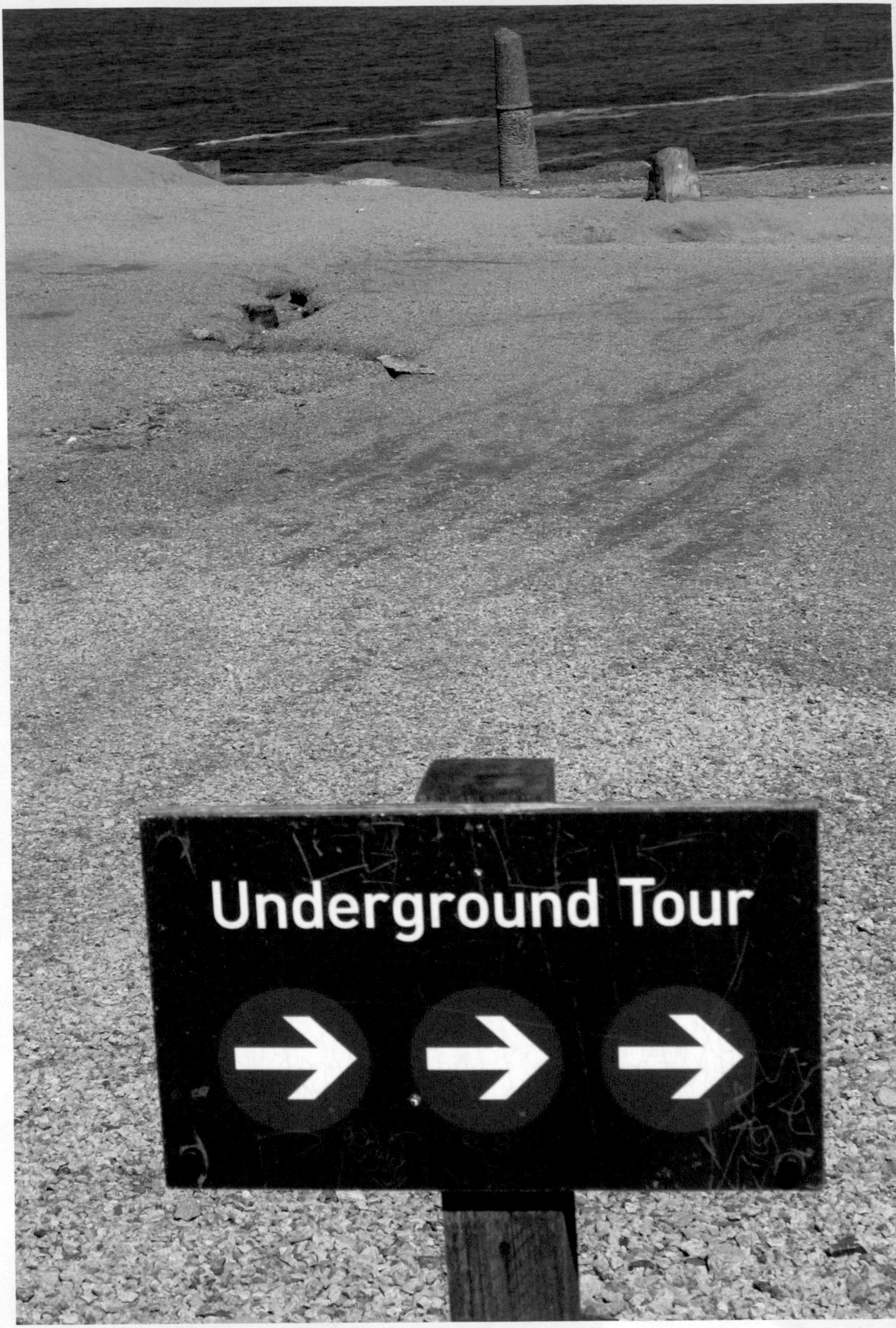
Underground Tour

INDEX

PHOTO CREDITS

All photos by Peter Naldrett except the following:

7 – Getty/Westend61; 9 – Getty/Visit Britain/Daniel Bosworth; 10–11 – Getty/Robbie Shore; 12 – Gareth Lowe Photography; 13 – Gareth Lowe Photography; 15 – Gareth Lowe Photography; 17 – The Beatles Story; 19 – The Beatles Story; 20 – The Beatles Story; 21 – Western Approaches; 22 (left) – Western Approaches; 23 – Western Approaches; 25 – Standedge Tunnel; 28 – Standedge Tunnel; 29 – Standedge Tunnel; 30 – National Coal Mining Museum for England; 32 – National Coal Mining Museum for England; 33 – National Coal Mining Museum for England; 34 – Rick Liguz; 35 – Rick Liguz; 37 – Rick Liguz; 38 – White Scar Caves; 39 – White Star Caves; 41 – Robbie Shone; 42 – White Scar Caves; 44–5 – Getty/Chris Howes; 49 – Victoria Tunnel; 51 – Victoria Tunnel; 52 – Victoria Tunnel; 53 – Beamish Museum; 54 – Beamish Museum; 55 – Beamish Museum; 56 – Beamish Museum; 57 – Beamish Museum; 58 – English Heritage; 60 – English Heritage; 62 – Jorvik Viking Centre; 63 – Jorvik Viking Centre; 64 – Jorvik Viking Centre; 65 – Jorvik Viking Centre; 66 – Jorvik Viking Centre; 67 – Jorvik Viking Centre; 68–9 – Peak Cavern; 70 – Getty/ Hauke Dressler/LOOK-foto; 71 – Ironbridge Museums; 73 – Ironbridge Museums; 74 – Robbie Shone; 76 – Poole's Cavern; 77 – Robbie Shone; 83 – Speedwell Cavern; 84 – Speedwell Cavern; 85 – Speedwell Cavern; 86 – Speedwell Cavern; 88 – Peak Cavern; 89 – Peak Cavern; 90 – Peak Cavern; 91 – Peak Cavern; 96 – Paul Kaye; 97 – Paul Kaye; 98 – Paul Kaye; 100–1 – Getty/Heritage Images; 102 – English Heritage; 103 – English Heritage; 104 – English Heritage; 106 – Kelvedon Hatch Secret Nuclear Bunker; 109 – Kelvedon Hatch Secret Nuclear Bunker; 110 – Imperial War Museums; 111 – Imperial War Museums; 112 – Imperial War Museums; 113 – Jay Bergesen; 114 – Imperial War Museums; 115 – The Postal Museum; 117 – The Postal Museum; 119 – Historic Royal Palaces; 120 – Historic Royal Palaces; 123 – Leeds Castle Foundation; 124 – Leeds Castle Foundation; 125 – Leeds Castle Foundation; 127 – Leeds Castle Foundation; 128 – Ramsgate Tunnels; 131 – Ramsgate Tunnels; 132 – English Heritage; 135 – English Heritage; 136–7 – Getty/Matthew Lloyd/Stringer; 138 – Southern Water; 141 – Southern Water; 142–3 – Getty/oversnap; 144 – Bath & Northeast Somerset Council; 145 – Bath & Northeast Somerset Council; 146 – Bath & Northeast Somerset Council; 147 – Jonathan Eyers; 148 – Bath & Northeast Somerset Council; 149 – Jason Hawkes; 151 – cheddargorge.com; 152 – Nick Toornend; 153 – cheddargorge.com; 154 – Wookey Hole; 156 – Wookey Hole; 158–9 – Getty/Nick Cable; 160 – National Trust; 164 – John Scott; 166 – John Scott; 169 – Getty/kensorrie; 170 – Exeter Underground Passages; 172 – Exeter Underground Passages; 173 – Kents Cavern Prehistoric Caves; 174 – Kents Cavern Prehistoric Caves; 175 – Kents Cavern Prehistoric Caves; 177 – Kents Cavern Prehistoric Caves; 186 – Bernie Pettersen; 188 – Geevor Tin Mine; 190–1 – Llechwedd Slate Caverns; 192 – Cardiff Castle; 195 – Cardiff Castle; 196 –

GeoPictures.net; 197 – GeoPictures.net; 198–9 – GeoPictures.net; 200 – GeoPictures.net; 202 – Corris Mine Explorers; 203 – Corris Mine Explorers; 204 – Corris Mine Explorers; 205 – Corris Mine Explorers; 206 – Corris Mine Explorers; 207 – King Arthur's Labyrinth; 209 – King Arthur's Labyrinth; 210 – King Arthur's Labyrinth; 211 – King Arthur's Labyrinth; 212 – ZipWorld Caverns; 213 – ZipWorld Caverns; 214 – ZipWorld Caverns; 215 – ZipWorld Caverns; 216 – Llechwedd Slate Caverns; 217 – James Petts; 218–19 – Llechwedd Slate Caverns; 221 – Llechwedd Slate Caverns; 222 – Go Below Underground Adventures; 223 – Go Below Underground Adventures; 224 – Go Below Underground Adventures; 225 – Go Below Underground Adventures; 226 – Great Orme Mines; 227 – Great Orme Mines; 229 – Great Orme Mines; 230–1 – Scotland's Secret Bunker; 232 – The Real Mary King's Close; 233 – The Real Mary King's Close; 234 – The Real Mary King's Close; 236 – The Real Mary King's Close; 237 – Mercat Tours; 238 – Mercat Tours; 239 – Mercat Tours; 241 – Mercat Tours; 242 – Scotland's Secret Bunker; 245 – Scotland's Secret Bunker; 247 – Alex Mitchell; 249 – Alex Mitchell; 255 – Neil Holt

ACKNOWLEDGEMENTS

I would like to thank Nicola for being so lovely and supportive throughout this project, Toby for relishing each underground adventure, and Willow for coming around to the idea eventually. Thanks also to Mandy, who got stuck with me in a mine-shaft cage, and Neil, who was much better than me at subterranean caving. Bingham and Jo were very brave in the cavern – thank you for coming along. I am also extremely grateful to all the attractions featured in this book and to their wonderful tour guides for being so welcoming and informative while I was beneath Britain.

ABOUT THE AUTHOR

Adventures underground were not unusual for Peter Naldrett when he was growing up close to the Peak District. Speedwell Cavern, Treak Cliff Cavern and Peak Cavern were all within easy reach, and popular days out that opened his eyes to the wealth of travel opportunities available beneath our feet. A keen interest in geography and geology throughout school, college and university ensured his fascination with rocks, minerals and fossils continued.

When above ground, Peter writes for several magazines and newspapers on topics related to travel and the outdoors. He has written several books about the Peak District, Lake District and Yorkshire Dales, as well as contributing to teaching resources for Oxford University Press and online publisher Twinkl. He also goes into schools, inspiring the next generation of explorers.

He still lives on the edge of the Peak District, where he is kept on his toes by two of his fiercest critics – his adventurous children Toby and Willow.

He is working on two more books for Bloomsbury: a unique guide to the British coastline, and an explorer's handbook for 200 of the most beautiful and intriguing islands around Britain.